# PSYCHOANALYSIS AND RELIGION:
# A BIBLIOGRAPHY

by

Benjamin Beit-Hallahmi
(University of Haifa)

*NORWOOD EDITIONS*
*NORWOOD, PA.*

1980

© Copyright 1978 by Benjamin Beit-Hallahmi

Designed and Typeset by Mark Weiman

# CONTENTS.

**Introduction.**

**How To Use This Bibliography.**

**Subject Listings :**
1. Bibliographies.
2. Periodical reviews.
3. Freud On Religion : The Original Writings.
4. Freud On Religion : Additional Sources.
5. General Discussions and Critical Reviews.
6. African Religions.
7. Amerindian and Eskimo religions.
8. Ancient Near East Religions.
9. Buddhism and Hinduism.
10. Christianity - General.
11. Christianity - Artifacts.
12. Christianity - Dogma.
13. Christianity - Holidays and Festivals.
14. Christianity - Mythology.
15. Christianity - Ritual.
16. Christianity - Sects.
17. "Primitive" religion.
18. Greek Religion and Mythology.
19. Islam.
20. Judaism - General.
21. Judaism - Artifacts.
22. Judaism - Dogma.
23. Judaism - Holidays and Festivals.

24. Judaism - Mythology.
25. Judaism - Ritual.
26. Freud, Judaism, and Psychoanalysis.
27. Mythology - General and Comparative.
28. Origins of Religion.
29. Prehistorical Religions.
30. Religion, Personality, and Psychopathology.
31. Religious Thinking and Religious Experience.
32. Ritual - General.
33. Contemporary Cults, Spiritualism, and Magic.
34. Ego Psychology and the psychology of Religion.
35. Object Relations Theory and the Psychology of Religion.
36. Totemism.
37. Academic ("Empirical") Studies.
38. Attempts to Reconcile Psychoanalysis and Religion.
39. Psychoanalytic Influences on Pastoral Counseling.

**Key To Subject Listings.**

**Alphabetical Listing and Index.**

# INTRODUCTION.

Psychoanalysis has produced more writings dealing with religion than any other psychological theory. Starting with the writings of Sigmund Freud, psychoanalytic writers have produced hundreds of books and articles, studying the origins, function and content of religion, and delving in the process into history, anthropology and religious literature. The aim of this bibliography is to guide the reader through this literature, and its creation has involved several choice points and decisions.

The first boundary that had to be marked off was that of psychoanalysis. This work covers those writers that follow psychoanalysis as formulated by Freud and his recognized disciples (and those writers reviewing this approach or criticizing it in their scholarly writings). Thus, what is covered is not "depth psychology", but psychoanalytic psychology. Works inspired by the theories of Jung and Adler were not included. The theoretical orientation of a publication served as the criterion, and not just a few key words. Not every writer suggesting a link between sexual motives and religion is a Freudian; most ofter he is not. Not every writer discussing "unconscious" elements in religion is a follower of psychoanalysis. One way of determining a theoretical bent is by examining the source of a publication and refences to it in other publications. Scholars familiar with psychoanalytic literature can easily name those journals that are more or less orthodox, and those which are outside the mainstream or beyond the pale. By analyzing citations one can also learn much about theoretical similarities and continuities.

The second boundary that had to be marked was that of content. How do we define religion and what kind of reference to it in a publication are we content with? The decision was rather conservative. Works dealing with folklore and superstition as their main topic were excluded. "Religion" was defined as a belief system which includes the notion of supernatural or divine beings. An attempt was made to include works which had religion as their main topic. Sources which contained passing references to religious matters were not included, except when such a reference has been especially important or seminal in stimulating further work. Thus, most works included are attempts to relate religion and psychoanalysis in a meaningful way.

The loss in terms of comprehensive inclusion has been a gain, it is hoped, in terms of consistency and significance. Reviewing some of the available bibliographies, it was discovered that very often classification of an entry has been based on its title, and not on its content. Certain key words in the title were sufficient for the classification of a book or an article, the result sometimes being totally erroneous. Our attempt to improve is not claimed to be completely successful, of course, since no bibliography is ever perfect.

The literature covered here is mostly in English, with the remainder in French. This creates an obvious limitation, since significant works in this field have been written in other languages, notably German. This limitation, however, has been overcome in most cases, with English translations being readily available. Like other fields in psychoanalysis, this one has seen the historical change from German to English over the years.

To summarize, one might say that our guidelines in creating this bibliography have been selectivity and significance. The classification of entries has been by content and not just by title.

A bibliography is a working tool, and we have tried to present a helpful tool. Our intended users for the bibliography include scholars and students in the fields of psychoanalysis, religion, anthropology, literature, folklore, sociology and history. We hope that the scholars using it will improve it even further in their own work.

The preparation of this bibliography has been helped by both institutions and individuals. I would like to acknowledge the support given by the Social Science Research Committee at the University of Haifa, and by the Graduate School of Education, University of Pennsylvania, where the work was completed. Ora Kauffman provided valuable technical assistance, and Jerome Weiman provided much appreciated interest and encouragement.

## HOW TO USE THIS BIBLIOGRAPHY.

Each entry included in the bibliography is listed at least twice: once under a subject heading and once again in the alphabetical listing section. The alphabetical listing section is also indexed.

If you are looking for references related to a subject, you should start with the Table of Contents, and determine the subject closest to your interest. Subject classifications for entries are neither exhaustive nor exclusive. They are based on the major topics covered in the entry. Thus, the same entry may appear under more than one subject heading.

From the subject listings it is possible to construct specialized reference lists. The Alphabetical listing is your best source if you are interested in the writings of an individual, or want to check a partial reference.

Examples: If you are interested in material on Christmas, look under "Christianity - Holidays and Festivals." If you are interested in all of Erik Erikson's publications dealing with religion, start with the alphabetical listing. You can then find out what specific subjects they relate to.

The references follow the American Psychological Association style for citations as much as possible. The elements in a reference entry are arranged in the following order:

Author: All authors, with surnames and initials (not full name) in inverted order.

Title: Article, chapter, or book.

Publication data: For journals - journal name in full, date of publication, volume number, inclusive pages. For books - place of publication, publisher's name, publication date.

## 1. BIBLIOGRAPHIES.

Capps, D., Rambo, L. & Ransohoff, P. *Psychology of Religion: A Guide to Information Sources.* Detroit: Gale, 1976.

Grinstein, A. *The Index of Psychoanalytic Writings.* New York: International Universities Press, 1956 - 1966, 1973.

Grinstein, A. *Sigmund Freud's Writings: A Comprehensive Bibliography.* New York: International Universities Press, 1977.

Kiell, N. *Psychoanalysis, Psychology and Literature: A Bibliography.* Madison: The University of Wisconsin Press, 1963.

Meissner, W. W. *Annotated Bibliography in Religion and Psychology.* New York: The Academy of Religion and Mental Health, 1961.

## 2. PERIODICAL REVIEWS.

Almansi, R. J. Applied psychoanalysis : Religion, mythology and folklore. In J. Frosch (Ed.) *The Annual Survey of Psychoanalysis*, 1953, *4*, 340-355.

Almansi, R. J. Applied psychoanalysis : Religion, mythology and folklore. In J. Frosch (Ed.) *The Annual Survey of Psychoanalysis*, 1954, *5*, 438-457.

Almansi, R. J. Applied psychoanalysis, I: Mythology and folklore. In J. Frosch (Ed.) *The Annual Survey of Psychoanalysis*, 1956, *7*, 376-383.

Almansi, R. J. Applied psychoanalysis, I: Religion, mythology and folklore. In. J. Frosch (Ed.) *The Annual Survey of Psychoananlysis*, 1957, *8*, 296-310.

Almansi, R. J. Applied psychoanalysis, I: Religion, mythology and folklore. In J. Frosch (Ed.) *The Annual Review of Psychoanalysis*, 1958, *9*, 439-449.

Arlow, J. A. Applied psychoanalysis: Religion. In J. Frosch (Ed.) *The Annual Survey of Psychoanalysis*, 1951, *2*, 538-553.

Cronbach, A. Psychoanalysis and religion. *Journal of Religion*, 1922, *2*, 588-599.

Cronbach, A. Religion and psychoanalysis. *Psychological Bulletin*, 1926, *23*, 701-713.

Cronbach, A. The psychology of religion: A bibliographical survey. *Psychological Bulletin*, 1928, *25*, 701-719.

Cronbach, A. The psychology of religion. *Psychological Bulletin*, 1933, *30*, 327-361.

Hopkins, P. A. A critical survey of the psychologies of religion. *Character and Personality*, 1937, *6*, 16-35.

Reik, T. Mythology (Collected Reviews). *International Journal of Psycho-Analysis*, 1921, *2*, 101-105.

Saffady, W. New developments in the psychoanalytic study of religion: A bibliographical survey of the literature since 1960. *The Psychoanalytic Review*, 1976, *63*, 291-299.

Tarachow, S. Applied psychoanalysis: Religion. In J. Frosch (Ed.) *The Annual Survey of Psychoanalysis*, 1950, *1*, 312-317.

Tarachow, S. Mythology. In J. Frosch (Ed.) *The Annual Review of Psychoanalysis*, 1950, *1*, 317-321.

Tarachow, S. Applied psychoanalysis: Mythology and folklore. In J. Frosch (Ed.) *The Annual Survey of Psychoanalysis*, 1951, *2*, 553-567.

Tarachow, S. Applied psychoanalysis: Religion and mythology. In J. Frosch (Ed.) *The Annual Survey of Psychoanalysis*, 1952, *3*, 494-511.

# 3. FREUD ON RELIGION : THE ORIGINAL WRITINGS.

In *The Standard Edition of the Complete Psychological Works of Sigmund Freud*. (J. Strachey, Ed.). London: The Hogarth Press, 1953-1974. Entries listed according to date of original writing and volume.

| | |
|---|---|
| 1893a | On the psychical mechanism of hysterical phenomena: Preliminary communication. *2*, 1-18, 1955. |
| 1893b | Charcot. *3*, 7-24, 1962. |
| 1901 | *The Psychopathology of Everyday Life*. *6*, 1-290, 1960. |
| 1905 | Fragment on an analysis of a case of hysteria. *7*, 1-122, 1953. |
| 1907 | Obsessive actions and religious practices. *9*, 116-129, 1959. |
| 1909a | Analysis of a phobia in a five-year-old boy. *10*, 1-150, 1955. |
| 1909b | Notes upon a case of obsessional neurosis. *10*, 151-318, 1955. |
| 1910a | *Leonardo da Vinci and a Memory of His Childhood*. *11*, 59-138, 1957. |
| 1910b | The future prospects of psychoanalytic therapy, *11*, 139-152, 1957. |
| 1911a | Psychoanalytic notes on a autobiographical account of a case of paranoia (Dementia Paranoides). *12*, 1-84, 1958. |
| 1911b | Formulations on the two principles of mental functioning. *12*, 213-226. |
| 1911c | 'Great is Diana of the Ephesians'. *12*, 342-344. 1958. |
| 1913 | *Totem and Taboo*. *13*, 1-164, 1955. |

| | |
|---|---|
| 1914a | The Moses of Michaelangelo. *13*, 211-236. |
| 1914b | On the history of the psychoanalytic movement. *14*, 1-66, 1957. |
| 1915 | Thoughts for the time on war and death. *14*, 273-300, 1957. |
| 1918 | From the history of an infantile neurosis. *17*, 1-122. |
| 1919 | Psychoanalysis and religious origins. Preface to T. Reik, *Ritual: Psychoanalytic Studies*. 17, 257-266, 1955. |
| 1921 | *Group Pychology and the Analysis of the Ego. 18*, 65-144, 1955. |
| 1923a | The ego and the id. *19*, 1-59, 1961. |
| 1923b | A seventeenth-century demonological neurosis., *19*, 67-108, 1961. |
| 1924 | A short account of psycho-analysis. *19*, 191-212, 1961. |
| 1925 | An autobiographical study. *20*, 1-74, 1959. |
| 1927 | *The Future of An Illusion. 21*, 1-56, 1961. |
| 1928a | Dostoevsky and parricide. *21*, 177-196, 1961. |
| 1928b | A religious experience. *21*, 167-174, 1961. |
| 1930 | *Civilization and Its Discontents. 21*, 57-146, 1961. |
| 1932 | The acquisition and control of fire. *22*, 183-194, 1964. |
| 1933 | *New Introductory Lectures On Psychoanalysis. 22*, 1-182, 1964. |
| 1939 | *Moses and Monotheism. 23*, 1-138, 1964. |

## 4. FREUD ON RELIGION : ADDITIONAL SOURCES.

Binswanger, L. *Sigmund Freud: Reminiscences of a Friendship.* New York. Grune & Stratton, 1957.

Fisher, D. J. Sigmund Freud and Romain Rolland: The terrestrial animal and his great oceanic friend. *American Imago,* 1976, *33,* 1-59.

Freud, E. L. Reply to M. Naftalin, Footnote to the genesis of Moses. In *The Psychoanalytic Quarterly,* 1958, *27,* 403-405. *The Psychoanalytic Quarterly,* 1959, *28,* 146.

Grinstein, A. *Sigmund Freud's Writings: A Comprehensive Bibliography.* New York: International Universities Press, 1977.

Jones, E. *The Life and Work of Sigmund Freud.* New York: Basic Books, 1953.

Meng, H, & Freud, E. L. (Eds.) *Psychoanalysis and Faith: The Letters of Sigmund Freud and Oskar Pfister.* New York: Basic Books, 1963.

Pruyser, P. W. Sigmund Freud and his legacy. In C. Y. Glock & P. E. Hammond (Eds.) *Beyond the Classics? Essays in the Scientific Study of Religion.* New York: Harper & Row, 1973.

See also sections 5, 26.

## 5. GENERAL DISCUSSIONS AND CRITICAL REVIEWS.

Apolito, A. Psychoanalysis and religion. *American Journal of Psychoanalysis*, 1970, *30*, 115-126.

Bakan, D. *Disease, Pain, and Sacrifice: Toward a Psychology of Suffering*. Chicago: University of Chicago Press, 1968, 134p.

Bakan, D. *The Duality of Human Existence*. Chicago: Rand McNally, 1966.

Banks, R. Religion as Projection. *Religious Studies*, 1973, *9*, 401-426.

Baudouin, C. *Psychanalyse de Symbole Religieuse*. Paris: Fayard, 1957.

Beirnaert, R. P. L. Psychanalyse et symbolisme religieux (Psychoanalysis and religious symbolism). *Cahiers Laennec*, 1948, *8*, 42-50.

Beirnaert, Louis. Freud, la religion et la civilisation (Freud, religion, and civilization). In *Problemes de Psychanalyse*, Paris. Fayard, 1957, 173-183.

Beit-Hallahmi, B. and Argyle, M. God as a father projection: The theory and the evidence. *British Journal of Medical Psychology*, 1975, *48*, 71-75.

Bidney, D. So-called primitive medicine and religion. In I. Gladston (Ed.) *Man's Image in Medicine and Anthropology*. New York: International Universities Press, 1963.

Blum, F. H. Psychoanalysis and religion (an historical view of Freud). In Wolff W. *Psychiatry and Religion*. New York: MD Publications, 1955, 8-13.

Boas, F. The methods of ethnology. *American Anthropologist*, New Series 1920, *22*, 315-321.

Bonaparte, M. Psycho-analysis in relation to social, religious and natural forces. *International Journal of Psycho-Analysis*, 1958, *39*, 513-515.

Brandt, R. J. Freud and Nietzsche: A comparison. *Review of the University of Ottawa*, 1955, *25*, 225-234.

Brenner, C. *An Elementary Textbook of Psychoanalysis*. Garden City, New York: Doubleday, 1974.

Brodbeck, A. J. Religion and art as socializing agencies: A note on the revision of Marxist and Freudian theories. *Psychological Reports*, 1957, *3*, 161-165.

Brown, N. O. *Life Against Death*. Middletown, Connecticut: Wesleyan University Press, 1958.

Brown, N. O. *Love's Body*. New York: Random House, 1966.

Bunker, H. A. Psychoanalysis and the study of religion. In G. Roheim (ed.) *Psychoanalysis and the Social Sciences*. Vol. III. New York: International Universities Press, 1951.

Burke, K. *The Rhetoric of Religion: Studies in Logology*. Boston: Beacon Press, 1961, vi + 327 p.

Caprio, S. Ethnological attitudes toward death: a psychoanalytic evaluation. *Journal of Clinical Psychopathology*, 1946, 7, 737-752.

Casey, R. P. The psychoanalytic study of religion. *Journal of Abnormal and Social Psychology*, 1938, *33*, 437-452.

Casey, R. P. Psychoanalytic study of religion. In Strunk, O. *Readings in the Psychology of Religion*. New York, Abingdon Press, 1959, 62-74.

Chassel, J. O. Freudianism and religion. *Methodist Rev.*, 1922, July, 507-524.

Cohen, M. B. Psychoanalysis and religion. *Psychiatry*, 1952, *15*, 219-220.

Cole, W. G. *Sex in Christianity and Psychoanalysis*. New York, London: Oxford University Press, 1966, xvi + 329 p.

Condon, W. S. Psychoanalysis and civilization. *Psychiatric Commentary*, 1960, *3*, 5-20.

Coster, G. *Psychoanalysis for Normal People*. London: Oxford University Press, 1926, 1927, 232 p.: 1942, viii + 227 p.

Dare, C. An aspect of the ego psychology of religion: A comment on Dr. Guntrip's paper. *British Journal of Medical Psychology*, 1969, *42* 335-340.

Day, F. The future of psychoanalysis and religion. *The Psychoanalytic Quarterly*, 1944, *13*, 84-92.

Dillistone, F. W. *Christianity and Symbolism*. London: Collins 1955, 320 p.

Dorsey, J. M. Some considerations of the psychoanalytical principle and religious living. *Samiksa*, 1954, *8*, 47-57: 93-124.

Eissler, K. R. Appendix 2. Further notes on the religious controversy. In *Medical Orthodoxy and the Future of Psychoanalysis*. New York: International Universities Press, 1965.

Eliade, M. *Images and Symbols: Studies in Religious Symbolism*. (Tr. Mairet, P.) New York: Sheed & Ward, 1961, 189 p.

Erikson, E. H. *Childhood and Society*. 2nd Ed. New York: Norton, 1963.

Farrell, B. A. Psychological theory and the belief in God. *International Journal of Psycho-Analysis*, 1955, *36*, 187-204.

Feiner, A. H. and Levenson, E. A. The compassionate sacrifice: An explanation of a metaphor. *The Psychoanalytic Review*, 1968-69, *55*, 552-573.

Feldman, A. B. Freudian theology. Part I. *Psychoanalysis*, 1952, *1*, (1), 31-52.

Feldman, A. B. Freudian theology. Part II. *Psychoanalysis*, 1953, *1*, (2), 37-53.

Fisher, D. J. Sigmund Freud and Romain Rolland: The terrestrial animal and his great oceanic friend. *American Imago*, 1976, *33*, 1-59.

Flugel, J. C. *Man, Morals and Society*. New York: International Universities Press, 1945.

Franzblau, A. N. Psychiatry and religion. In Noveck, S. (Ed.) Judaism and Psychiatry, 183-192.

Freeman, D. Thunder, blood and nicknaming God's creatures. *The Psychoanalytic Quarterly*, 1968, *37*, 353-399.

Fromm, E. *Psychoanalysis and Religion*. New Haven Yale, 1950.

Fromm, E. *The Dogma of Christ and Other Essays on Religion, Psychology and Culture*. London: Routledge, 1963, 151 p. New York / Chicago / San Francisco: Holt Rinehart & Winston, 1963, 1964, x + 212 p. New York: Doubleday, 1966, ix + 213 p.

Glover, E. *Freud or Jung*. New York: Norton, 1950.

Guntrip, H. J. S. Religion in relation to personal integration. *British Journal of Medical Psychology*, 1969, *42*, 323-333.

Held, R. R. Religion, rationalisme et psychanalyse (Religion, rationalism and psychoanalysis). In *Les Cahiers Rationalistes*. Paris: Union Rationaliste, 1959.

Held, R. R. Contribution a l'etude psychanalytique du phenomene religieus (Contribution to the psychoanalytic study of the religious phenomenon). *Revue Francaise de Psychanalyse*, 1962, *26*, 211-266.

Herberg, W. Freud, religion and social reality "The incomprehensible monster, Man." *Commentary*, 1957, *23*, 277-284.

Hiltner, S. The psychological understanding of religion. In Strunk, O., Jr. (Ed. ) *Readings in the Psychology of Religion*. Nashville, Tennessee: Abingdon Press, 1959, 74-104.

Hiltner, S. Religion and psychoanalysis. *Psychoanalytic Review*, 1950, *37*, 128 - 139.

Hinkle, B. M. The spiritual significance of psychoanalysis. *British Journal of Psychology*, 1921-22, *2*, 209-230.

Hinsie, L. I. Psychoanalysis and heaven. *Psychoanalytic Review*, 1926, *13*, 145-172.

Homans, P. Toward a psychology of religion by way of Freud and Tillich. *Zygon*, 1967, *2*, 97-119.

Homans, P. *Theology after Freud*, Indianapolis: Bobbs-Merrill, 1970.

Hopkins, P. A critical survey of the psychologies of religion. *Character and Personality*, 1937, *6*, 16-35.

Hora, T. Psychotherapy, existence and religion. *Psychoanalysis and the Psychoanalytic Review*, 1959, *46*, 91-98.

Isenberg, M Morality and the neurotic patient. *American Journal of Psychotherapy*, 1966, *20*, 477-488.

Jahoda, G. *The Psychology of Superstition.* Baltimore; Penguin Books, 1969, 158 p.

Jones, E. The symbolic significance of salt in folklore and superstition. In Jones, E. *Essays in Applied Psycho-Analysis.* London, Vienna- International Psychoanalytic Press, 1923, 112-203. London: The Hogarth Press and the Institute of Psycho-Analysis, 1951, *2*, 22-109.

Jones, E. The psychology of religion. *British Journal of Medical Psychology*, 1926, *6*. 265-269.    In Jones, E. *Essays in Applied Psychoanalysis.* London, Vienna- International Psychoanalytic Press, 1923. London: The Hogarth Press and the Institute of Psycho-Analysis, 1951, 190-197.

Jones, E. Psychoanalysis and the psychologyof religion In Lorand Sandor (Ed.) *Psychoanalysis Today.* New York: Covici-Friede, 1933, 323-337. Under title: The psychology of religion. Lorand Sandor (Ed.) *Psychoanalysis Today.* New York: International Universities Press, 1944, 315-325.

Jones, E. *Essays in Applied Psychoanalysis. Vol. II. Essays in Folklore, Anthropology and Religion..* London: Hogarth Press, 1951.

Kamiat, A. H The cosmic phantasy. *Psychoanalytic Review*, 1928, *15*, 210-219.

Kaplan, L. The belief inwitches and in magic (A psychoanalytic study). *J. Sexol. Psychanal., 1923, 1,* 349-363.

Kiev, A. Primitive religious rites and behavior: Clinical considerations. *International Psychiatry Clinics,* 1969, *5,* 119-131.

Klauber, J. The present status of Freud's views of religion. *Synagogue Review,* 1960, *34,* 219-225.

Klausner, S. Z. Sacred and profane meanings of blood and alcohol. *Journal of Social Psychology*, 1964, *64*, 27-43.

Kleinschmidt, H. J. Beyond Philip Rieff: The triumph of Sigmund Freud. *American Imago*, 1966, *23*, 244-256.

Klibansky, R. Panofsky, E. and Saxl F. *Saturn and Melancholy. Studies in the History of Natural Philosophy, Religion and Art.* New York: Basic Books, 1964, 429 p.

Kristol, I. God and the psychoanalyst. *Commentary*, 1949, *8*, 434-443.

La Barre, W. The influence of Freud on anthropology. *American Imago*, 1958, *15*, 276-328.

La Barre, W. Religions, Rorschachs and tranquilizers. *American Journal of Orthopsychiatry*, 1959, *29*, 688-698.

La Barre, W. *The Human Animal*. Chicago: University of Chicago Press, 1949.

La Barre, W. *The Ghost Dance: The origins of Religion.* New York: Doubleday, 1970.

Laguna, F. de. Method and theory of ethnology. In author's *American Anthropologist: Selected Papers*, 1888-1920. Evanston, Illinois: Row, Peterson, 1960, 782-792.

Lederer, W. Dragons, delinquents, and destiny: An essay on positive superego functions. *Psychological Issues, No. 15.* New York: International Universities Press, 1964.

Lubin, A. J. A psychoanalytic view of religion. In E. M. Pattison (Ed.) *Clinical Psychiatry and Religion.* Boston: Little, Brown & Company, 1969.

Lussheimer, P. Psychoanalysis and religion. *American Journal of Psychoanalysis*, 1953, *18*, 88.

Mann, J. (Reporter) Panel on clinical and theoretical aspects of religious belief (Read at Am Psa Ass., May 1963). *Journal of the American Psychoanalytic Association*, 1964, *12*, 160-170.

Mannoni, O. *Freud.* New York: Pantheon, 1971.

Marmorston, J., Stainbrook, E. (Ed.) *Psychoanalysis and the Human Situation.* New York / Washington / Hollywood: Vantage Press, 1964, 270 p.

Masih, Y. *Freudianism and Religion.* Calcutta: Thacker Spink, 1964, 356 p.

McClelland, C. *The Roots of Consciousness.* Princeton, New Jersey. Van Nostrand, 1964, v + 219 p.

Miura, T. Psychoanalysis and religion. *The Japanese Journal of Psycho-Analysis,* 1955, *2,* 5-10.

Moloney, J. C. Mother, God and superego. *Journal of the American Psychoanalytic Association,* 1954, *2,* 120-151.

Money-Kryle, R. E. *Religion in a Changing World.* London: Watts & Company: The Rationalist Annual, 1948.

Moxon, C. Religion in the light of psycho-analysis. *Psychoanalytic Review,* 1921, *8,* 92-98.

Moxon, Cavendish. *Freudian Essays in Religion and Science.* Boston. Badger, 1927.

Moxon, C. Freud's denial of religion. *British Journal of Medical Psychology,* 1931, *11,* 150-157.

Naumburg, M. Religious symbols in the unconscious of man. *International Record of Medicine,* 1958, *17,* 723-731.

Nelson, B. N. The future of illusions. *Psychoanalysis,* 1951, *2,* 16-37.

Ostow, M. Biological basis of religious symbolism. *International Record of Medicine,* 1958, *171,* 709-717.

Ostow, M. The nature of religious controls. *American Psychologist,* 1958, *13,* 571-574.

Ostow, M. Religion. In Arieti, S. (Ed.) *American Handbook of Psychiatry.* New York: Basic Books, 1966, II, 1789-1801.

Pasche, F. Freud et l'orthodoxie judeo - chretienne (Freud and Judeo - Christian orthodoxy). *Revue Francaise de Psychanalyse,* 1961, *25,* 55-87.

Paul, R. A. Did the primal crime take place? *Ethos,* 1976, *4,* 311-352.

Philp, H. L. *Freud and Religious Belief.* London: Rockliff, 1956.

Phipott, S. J. F. Unconscious mechanisms in religion. *British Journal of Medical Psychology* 1942, *19,* 292-312.

Postle, B. Religion in the psychologies of Jung and Freud. *Ohio State Medical Journal,* 1947, *43,* 947-950.

Pruyser, P. W. *A Dynamic Psychology of Religion.* New York: Harper & Row, 1968.

Pruyser, P. W. Sigmund Freud and his legacy: Psychoanalytic psychology of religion. In C. Y. Glock and P. E. Hammond (Eds.) *Beyond the Classics? Essays in the Scientific Study of Religion.* New York: Harper & Row, 1973.

Racker, E. (Heinrich) On Freud's position towards religion. *Americam Imago,* 1956, *13*, 97-121.

Rank, O. and Sachs, H. The significance of psychoanalysis for the humanities. *American Imago*, 1964, *21*, 7-128.

Reik, T. The therapy of the neuroses and religion. *International Journal of Psycho-Analysis,* 1929, *10*, 292-302.

Rickets, M. L. Anthropological psychoanalysis of religion. *History of Religions,* 1971, *11*, 147-156.

Ricoeur, P. The atheism of Freudian psychoanalysis. *Concilium,* 1966, *16*, 59-72.

Ricoeur, P. *Freud and Philosophy- An Essay on Interpretation.* New Haven: Yale University Press, 1971, xv + 573 p.

Rieff, P. *Freud: The Mind of the Moralist.* New York: Viking Press, 1959.

Rieff, P. The meaning of history and religion in Freud's thought. In B. Mazlish (Ed.) *Psychoanalysis and History.* Englewood Cliffs, N. J. . Prentice-Hall, 1963.

Rieff, P. *The Triumph of the Therapeutic.* New York: Harper & Row, 1966.

Reisman, D. Freud: Religion as Neurosis. *University of Chicago Round Table,* 1950, No. 638, 13-20.

Reisman, D. Freud, religion and science. *American Scholar,* 1951, *20*, 267-276.

Roheim, G. The psycho-analytic interpretation of culture. *International Journal of Psychoanalysis,* 1941, *22*, 147-169.

Roheim, G. The Oedipus complex, magic and culture. *Psychoanalysis and the Social Sciences,* 1950, *2*, 173-228.

Ross, N. Psychoanalysis and religion. *Journal of the American Psychoanalytic Association*, 1958, *6*, 519-539.

Ross, N. Beyond "The Future of an illusion." *Journal of the Hillside Hospital*, 1968, *17*, 259-276.

de Rougemont, D. *The Devil's Share: An Essay on the Diabolic in Modern Society*. New York: Meridian Books, 1956.

Rubenstein, R. L. A note on the research lag in psychoanalytic studies in religion. *Jewish Social Studies*, 1963, *25*, 133-144.

Saffady, W. New developments in the psychoanalytic study of religion. A bibliographic survey of the literature since 1960. *The Psychoanalytic Review*, 1976, *63*, 291-299.

Schmidl, F. Problems of methods in applied psychoanalysis. *Psychoanalytic Quarterly*, 1972, *41*, 402-419.

Sherman, M. H. Values, religion and the psychoanalyst. *Journal of Social Psychology*, 1957, *45*, 261-269.

Sillman, L. R. Monotheism and the sense of reality. *International Journal of Psychoanalysis*, 1949, *30*, 124-132.

Spinks, G. S. *Psychology and Religion: An Introduction to Contemporary Views*. Boston: Beacon Press, 1965, xv + 221 p.

Stephane, A. *L'univers Contestationnaire, ou les Nouveaux Chretiens: Etude Psychoanalytique* (The Universe in Contention, or the New Christians: Psychoanalytic Study). Paris: Payot, 1969.

Strunk, O., Jr. (Ed.) *Readings in the Psychology of Religion*. New York: Abingdon Press, 1959, 288 p.

Sullivan, J. J. Two psychologies and the study of religion. *Journal for the Scientific Study of Religion*, 1961-62, *1*, 155-164.

Swisher, W. S. *Religion and the New Psychology, a Psycho-Analytic Study of Religion*. Boston: Marshall Jones, 1920, xv + 261 p. London: Routledge, 1920, 286 p.

Taubes, J. Religion and the future of psychoanalysis. *Psychoanalysis*, 1956-57, *4 - 5*, 136 - 142.

Tillich, P. J. The religious symbol (Tr.: Adams, J. L. and Fraenkel, E.) *Daedalus*, 1958, *87*, 3 - 21.

Turner, J. E. Freud and the illusion of religion. *Journal of Religion*, 1933, *11*, 212-221.

Vetter, G. B. *Magic and Religion: Their Psychological Nature, Origin, and Function.* New York: Philosophical Library, 1958, 555p.

Wells, F. L. The beans of St. Botolph's: And other letters to Screwtape. *American Imago* 1948, *5*, 38-64.

Wile, I. S. Psychoanalysis and religion. *Mental Hygiene*, 1932, *16*, 529 - 563.

Wisdom, J. O. Gods. In Wisdom, J. O., *Philosophy and Psychoanalysis*. London: Blackwell, 1952, 149 - 168.

## 6. AFRICAN RELIGIONS.

Beidelman, T. O. The ox and Nuer sacrifice: Some Freudian hypotheses about Nuer symbolism. *Man*, 1966, *1*, 453 -467.

Fortes, M. *Oedipus and Job in West African Religion.* New York: Cambridge University Press, 1959.

Groves, E. R. Freudian elements in the animism of the Niger Delta. *The Psychoanalytic Review*, 1917, *4*, 333 - 338.

Prince, R. The Yoruba image of the witch. *British Journal of Psychiatry*, 1961, *107*, 795 - 805.

Prince, R. Indigenous Yoruba Psychiatry. In Kiev, A. *Magic, Faith and Healing.* Glencoe, Illinois: Free Press. London: Collier - Macmillan, 1964, 84 - 120.

## 7. AMERINDIAN AND ESKIMO RELIGIONS.

Barnes, F. F. The myth of the seal ancestors. *The Psychoanalytic Review*, 1953, *40*, 156 - 157.

Barnouw, V. A psychological interpretation of a Chippewa origin legend. *Journal of American Folklore*, 1955, *68*, 73 - 85, 211 - 223, 341 - 355.

Boyer, L. B. Stone as a symbol in Apache mythology. *American Imago*, 1965, *22*, 14 - 39.

Devereux, G. Dream learning and individual ritual differences in Mohave shamanism. *American Anthropologist*, 1957, *59*, 1036 - 1045.

Dundes, A. Earth diver: Creation of the mythopoeic male. *American Anthropologist*, 1962, *64*, 1032 - 1051.

Kaplan, B. Psychological themes in Zuni mythology and Zuni TAT's. *Psychoanalytic Study of Society*, 1962, *2*, 255 - 262.

La Barre, W. A cultist drug - addiction in an Indian alcoholic. *Bulletin of the Menninger Clinic*, 1941, *5*, 40 - 46.

La Barre, W. Primitive psychotherapy in native American cultures: Peyotism and confession. *Journal of Abnormal and Social Psychology*, 1947, *42*, 294 - 309.

La Barre, W. Confession as cathartic therapy in native American Indian tribes. In A. Kiev (Ed.) *Magic, Faith, and Healing*. New York: Free Press, 1964.

La Barre, W. *The Peyote Cult*. 2nd Ed. New York: Schocken Books, 1969.

Leighton, A. H. and Leighton, D. C. Elements of psychotherapy in Navaho religion. *Psychiatry*, 1941, *4*, 515 - 523.

Sarnoff, C. A. Mythic symbols in two precolumbian myths. *American Imago*, 1969, *26*, 3 - 20.

Skeels, D. R. Eros and thanatos in Nez Perce river mythology. *American Imago*, 1964, *21*, 103 - 110.

Spencer, K. *Mythology and Values. An Analysis of Navaho Chantway Myths*. Philadelphia: Amer. Folklore Soc., 1957, 240 p.

Walsh, M. N. A psychoanalytic interpretation of a primitive dramatic ritual. *Journal of the Hillside Hospital*, 1962, *11*, 3 - 20.

## 8: ANCIENT NEAR EAST RELIGIONS.

Abraham, K. Amenhotep IV: A psychoanalytic contribution to the understanding of his personality and the monotheistic cult of Athon. *Psychoanalytic Quarterly*, 1935, *4*, 537 - 569.

Brend, W. A. *Sacrifice to Attis. A study of Sex and Civilization.* London: Toronto : Heinemann, 1936, 350 p.

Chandler, T. Ikhnaton and Moses. *American Imago*, 1962, *19*, 127 - 139.

Coriat, I. H. A note on the sexual symbolism on the Cretan snake goddess. *Psychoanalytic Review*, 1917, *4*, 367 - 368.

Desmonde, W. H. The bull fight as a religious ritual. *American Imago*, 1952, *9*, 173 - 195.

Fodor, A. Asherah of Ugarit. *American Imago*, 1952, *9*, 118 - 146.

Freeman, T. Some notes on a forgotten religion. *The Psychoanalytic Review*, 1954, *41*, 9 - 28.

Gressot, M. Le mythe dogmatique et le systeme moral des Manicheens. *Revue Francaise de Psychanalyse*, 1953, *17*, 398 - 427.

Lederer, W. Oedipus and the serpent. *The Psychoanalytic Review*, 1964 - 65, *51*, 619 - 644.

Locke, N. A myth of ancient Egypt. *American Imago*, 1961, *18*, 105 - 128.

Moloney, J.C. Carnal myths involving the sun. *American Imago*, 1963, *20*, 93 - 104.

Pearson, G. H. J. A note on the medusa: A speculative attempt to expalin a ritual. *Bulletin of the Philadelphia Association for Psychoanalysis*, 1967, *17*, 1 - 9.

Pollock, R. E. Some psychoanalytic considerations of bullfighting and bull - worship. *Israel Annals of Psychiatry and Related Disciplines*, 1974, *12*, 53 - 67.

Reider, N. Chess, Oedipus and the Mater Dolorosa. *International Journal of Psycho-Analysis*, 1959, *40*, 515 - 528.

Roheim, G. Dying gods and puberty ceremonies. *Journal of the Royal Anthropological Institute*, 1929, *59*, 181 - 197.

Roheim, G. The panic of the gods. *The Psychoanalytic Quarterly*, 1952, *21*, 92 - 106.

Schneiderman, L. The cult of Osiris in relation to primitive initiation rites. *The Psychoanalytic Review*, 1965, *52*, 38 - 50.

Strachey. J. Preliminary notes upon the porblem of Akhnaten. *International Journal of Psychoanalysis*, 1939, *20*, 33 - 42.

Weigert-Vowinckel, E. The cult and mythology of the Magna Mater from the standpoint of psychoanalysis. *Psychiatry*, 1938, *1*, 347 - 378.

See also section 18.

## 9. BUDDHISM AND HINDUISM.

Alexander, F. Buddhistic training as an artificial catatonia. *The Psychoanalytic Review*, 1931, *18*, 129 - 145.

Bellah, R. N. Father and son in Christianity and Confucianism, *The Psychoanalytic Review*, 1965, *52*, 92 - 114.

Berkeley-Hill, O. The anal erotic factor in the religion, philosophy, and character of the Hindus. *International Journal of Psychoanalysis*, 1921, *2*, 306 - 338.

Chaudhuri, A. K. R. A psychoanalytic study of the Hindu mother goddess (Kali) concept. *American Imago*, 1956, *13*, 123 - 145.

Fromm, E. Psychoanalysis and Zen Buddhism. In D. T. Suzuki (Ed.) *Zen Buddhism and Psychoanalysis.* New York: Grove Press, 1963.

Halder, The Buddhist conception of personality as based on Abhidharmakosa of Vasubandhu. *Samiksa*, 1967, *21*, 55 - 56.

Hofling, C. K. Notes on Raychaudhuri's "Jesus Christ and Sir Krisna." *American Imago*, 1958, *15*, 213 - 226.

Kelman, H. Communing and relating. Part I. Past and current perspectives. *American Journal of Psychoanalysis*, 1958, *18*, 77 - 98.

Kondo, A. Intuition in Zen Buddhism. *American Journal of Psychoanalysis*, 1952, *12*, 10 - 14.

Leach, E. R. Pulleyar and the Lord Buddha: An aspect of religious syncretism in Ceylon. *Psychoanalysis and the Psychoanalytic Review*, 1962, *49*, 81 - 102.

Newell, H. W. An interpretation of the Hindu worship of Siva Linga. *Bulletin of the Philadelphia Association for Psychoanalysis*, 1954, *4*, 82 - 86.

Oyama, J. The theories of personality in psychoanalysis and the concept of the Three Consciousnesses (Vijnana) in Buddhism I. On Es and manovijanana. *American Journal of Psychoanalysis*, 1958, *5*, 9 - 14.

Oyama, J. Consideration of mental conflict and Adana-Vijnana. *Sendai Journal of Psychoanalysis*, 1953, 18 - 20.

Oyama, J. Comparative study on the psychoanalysis and Buddhism theory. *Sendai J. Psychoanal.*, 1953, 4 - 5.

Paul, R. A. The Sherpa temple as a model of the psyche. *American Ethnologist*, 1976, *3*, 131 - 146.

Paul, R. A. The eyes outnumber the nose two to one. *Psychoanalytic Review*, in press.

Paul, R. A. A mantra and its meaning. *The Psychoanalytic Study of Society*, in press.

Roychoudhuri, A. K. Sita myth of the Ramayana. *Samiska*, 1954, *8*, 235 - 243.

Schnier, J. The Tibetan Lamaist ritual: chod. *International Journal of Psycho-Analysis*, 1957, *38*, 402 - 407.

de Silva, M. W. P. *Buddhist and Freudian Psychology.* Colombo: Lake House Investment, 1973.

Stunkard, A. S. Some interpersonal aspects of an oriental religion. *Psychiatry*, 1951, *14*, 419 - 431.

Sun, J. T. Psychology in primitive Buddhism *The Psychoanalytic Review*, 1924, *11*, 39 - 47.

Suzuki, D. T. (ed.) *Zen Buddhism and Psychoanalysis.* New York: Grove Press, 1963.

Suzuki, D. T., Fromm, E. and De Martino, R. *Zen Buddhism and Psychoanalysis.* New York: Harper, 1960, viii + 180 p.

## 10. CHRISTIANITY - GENERAL

Bakan, D. *The Duality of Human Existence.* Chicago: Rand McNally, 1966.

Bonaparte, M. Eros, Saul de Tarse et Freud. *Revue Francaise de Psychanalyse,* 1957, *21*, 23 - 33.

Cohn, N. The cult of the free spirit: A medieval heresy reconstructed. *Psychoanalysis and the Psychoanalytic Review,* 1961, *48*, 51 - 68.

Freemantle, A. The Oedipal legend in Christian hagiology. *Psychoanalytic Quarterly,* 1950, *19*, 408 - 409.

Grollman, E. A. Some sights and insights of history, psychology and psychoanalysis concerning the Father-god and Mother-goddess concepts in Judaism and Christianity. *American Imago,* 1963, *20*, 187 - 209.

Holfing, C. K. Notes on Raychaudhuri's "Jesus Christ and Sir Krisna." *American Imago,* 1958, *15*, 213 - 226.

Jones, E. Psychoanalysis and the Christian religion. In Jones, E. *Essays in Applied Psychoanalysis.* London: The Hogarth Press and the Institute of Psychoanalysis, 1951, *2*, 198 - 211.

Klauber, J. Notes on the psychical roots of religion, with particular reference to the development of Western Christianity. *International Journal of Psychoanalysis,* 1974, *55*, 249 - 255.

Leavy, S. A. A religious conversion in a four year old girl: A historical note. *Bulletin of the Philadelphia Association for Psychoanalysis,* 1957, *7*, 85 - 90.

Leverenz, D. Shared fantasy in Puritan sermons. *American Imago,* 1975, *32*, 264 - 387.

Lidz, T. and Rothenberg, A. Psychedelism: Dyonysus reborn. *Psychiatry,* 1968, *31*, 116 - 125.

Lowenstein, R. M. *Christians and Jews.* New York: International Universities Press, 1951.

Reider, N. Chess, Oedipus and the Mater Dolorosa. *International Journal of Psychoanalysis,* 1959, *40*, 515 - 528.

Roheim, G. Saint Agatha and the Tuesday woman. *International Journal of Psycho-Analysis*, 1946, *27*, 119 - 126.

Sachs, H. At the gates of heaven. *American Imago*, 1947, *4*, 15 - 32.

Saffady, W. Fears of sexual licence during the English Reformation. *History of Childhood Quarterly*, 1973, *1*, 89 - 96.

Schick, A. The Jew as a sacrificial victim. *Psychoanalytic Review*, 1971, *58*, 75 - 89.

Schroeder, T. Guilt and inferiority as creator of religious experience. *The Psychoanalytic Review*, 1929, *16*, 46 - 54.

Suttie, I. D. Religion, racial character and mental and social health. *British Journal of Medical Psychology*, 1932, *12*, 289 - 314.

Tarachow, S. St. Paul and early Christianity. A psychoanalytic and historical study. In Muensterberger, W. and Axelrad S. *Psychoanalysis and the Social Sciences.* New York: International Universities Press, 1955, *4*, 223 - 282.

Wolf, R. Castration symbolism in patrisitic thought: Preliminary studies in the development of Christianity. *Psychoanalysis and the Psychoanalytic Review*, 1962, *49*, 26 - 38.

## 11. CHRISTIANITY - ARTIFACTS.

Watkins, J. G. Concerning Freud's paper on "The Moses of Michaelangelo." *American Imago*, 1951, *8*, 61 - 63.

## 12. CHRISTIANITY - DOGMA.

Cole, W. G. *Sex in Christianity and Psychoanalysis*, New York: Oxford University Press, 1966. xvi + 329 p.

Fromm, E. The dogma of Christ. In *The Dogma of Christ and Other Essays on Religion, Psychology and Culture.* New York: Holt, 1963, 3 - 91.

Homans, P. *Theology After Freud.* Indianapolis: Bobbs-Merrill, 1970.

Lowenfeld, H. The decline in belief in the devil: The consequence for group psychology. *The Psychoanalytic Quarterly*, 1969, *38*, 455-462.

Moxon, C. A psychoanalytic study of the Christian creed. *International Journal of Psychoanalysis*, 1931, *2*, 54 - 70.

Reik, T. *Dogma and Compulsion*, New York: International Universities Press, 1951.

## 13. CHRISTIANITY - HOLIDAYS AND FESTIVALS.

Baudouin, C. Signification des fetes (The meaning of festivities). *Psyche* - Paris, 1947, *2*, 1291-1308.

Beit-Hallahmi, B. Sacrifice, fire, and the victory of the sun: A search for the origins of Hanukkah. *The Psychoanalytic Review*, 1977, *63*, 497-509.

Bimer, L. The first foreign land. *Psychoanalytic Review*, 1971, *58*, 303 - 309.

Boyer, L. B. Christmas 'Neurosis'. *Journal of the American Psychoanalytic Association*, 1955, *3*, 467-488.

Eisenbud, J. Negative reactions to Christmas. *Psychoanalytic Quarterly*, 1941, *10*, 639-645.

Fraiberg, L. and Fraiberg, S. Hallowe'en: Ritual and myth in a children's holiday. *American Imago*, 1950, *7*, 289-327.

Jekels, L. The psychology of the festival of Christmas. *International Journal of Psychoanalysis*, 1936, *17*, 57-72.

Ramnoux, C. La fete du premier Novembre (The holiday of the first of November, the "All Saints" Day). *Psyche* - Paris, 1948, *3*, 1020-1040.

Reid, Robert E. Infantile crises associated with Christmas: A psychoanalytic interpretation. Dissertation Abstracts, 1968, *29*, (1-A), 321.

Sereno, R. Some observations on the Santa Claus Custom. *Psychiatry*, 1951, *14*, 387-396.

Sterba, R. A Dutch celebration of a festival. *American Imago*, 1941, *2*, 205-208.

Sterba, R. On Chirstmas. *Psychoanalytic Quarterly*, 1944, *13*, 79-83.

Sterba, R. On Hallowe'en. *American Imago*, 1948, *5*, 213-224.

## 14. CHRISTIANITY - MYTHOLOGY.


Arlow, J. A. The Madonna's conception through the ear. *The Psychoanalytic Study of Society*, 1964, *3*, 13-25.

Bellah, R. N. Father and son in Christianity and Confucianism. *The Psychoanalytic Review*, 1965, *52*, 92-114.

Badouin, C. Le Saint precepteur du Diable (The Saint tutor of the Devil). *Psyche* - Paris, 1949, *4*, 351-357.

Beirnaert, L. Le role affectif de la Vierge - Mere dans le catholicisme (The emotional role of the virgin-mother in Catholicism). *Psyche* - Paris, 1947, *2*, 1309-1318.

Bonaparte, M. Saint Christopher patron saint of the motor-car drivers. *American Imago*, 1947, *4*, 49-77.

Dundes, A. The father, the son and the holy Grail. *Literature and Psychology*, 1962, *12*, 101-112.

Dundes, A. The hero pattern and the life of Jesus. Colloquy 25. The center for Hermeneutical Studies. The Graduate Theological Union and the University of California, Berkeley. 1977.

Edelheit, H. Crucifixion fantasies and their relation to the primal scene. *International Journal of Psycho-Analysis*, 1974, *55*, 193-199.

Fodor, N. The hound of heaven. *Psychoanalysis*, 1955, *3*, 45-49.

de Groot, A. D. *Saint Nicholas: A Psychoanalytic Study of His History and Myth*. New York Basic Books, 1965.

Halpern, S. The man who forgot he crucified Jesus: An exegesis of Anatole France's "Procurator of Judea." *The Psychoanalytic Review*, 1964-65, *51*, 597-611.

Jacobs, L. I. The primal crime. *Psychoanalytic Review*, 1965, *52*, 456-484.

Jones, E. A psycho-analytical study of the Holy Ghost. In Jones, E. *Essays in Applied Psycho-Analysis*. London, Vienna. International Psychoanalytic Press 1923, 415-430.

Under title. A psychoanalytical study of the Holy Ghost concept. In *Essays in Applied Psychoanalysis*, The Hogarth Press and the Institute of Psychoanalysis, London, 1951, *2*, 353-373.

Jones, E. The Madonna's Conception through the ear - a contribution to the relation between aesthetics and religion. In author's *Essays in Applied Psycho-Analysis*. London, Vienna: International Psychoanalytic Press, 1923, 261-359. London: The Hogarth Press and the Institute of Psycho-Analysis, 1951, *2*, 266-357.

Lodge, A. Satan's symbolic syndrome: A psychological interpretation of Milton's Satan. *Psychoanalytic Review*, 1956, *43*, 411-422.

Parcells, F. H. & Segel, N. P. Oedipus and the Prodigal Son. *Psychoanalytic Quarterly*, 1959, *28*, 213-227.

Redl, F. Fritz Redl on "Den Heiligen Nikolaus." In Groot, A. de, *Saint Nicholas, A Psychoanalytic Study*. Hague: Mouton, 1965.

Reider, N. Medieval Oedipal legends about Judas. *Psychoanalytic Quarterly*, 1960, *29*, 515-527.

Schendler, D. Judas, Oedipus, and various saints. *Psychoanalysis*, 1954, *2*, 41-46.

Tarachow, S. Judas, the beloved executioner. *The Psychoanalytic Quarterly*, 1960, *29*, 528-554.

Wayne, R. Prometheus and Christ. *Psychoanalysis and the Social Sciences*, 1951, *3*, 201-219.

See also section 27.

## 15. CHRISTIANITY - RITUAL.

Schuster, D. B. The Holy Communion: An historical and psycho-analytic study. *The Bulletin of the Philadelphia Association for Psychoanalysis*, 1970, *20*, 223-236.

Tarachow, S. Totem feast in modern dress. *American Imago*, 1948, *5*, 65 -

Wayne, R. A little religious ceremonial. *American Imago*, 1954, *11*, 194-202.

See also section 13.

## 16. CHRISTIANITY - SECTS.

Feldman, A. B. Animal magnetism and the mother of Christian Science. *The Psychoanalytic Review*, 1963, *50*, 313-320.

La Barre, W. *They Shall Take Up Serpents.* Minneapolis: University of Minnesota Press, 1962.

Schroeder, T. A contribution to the psychology of religion: The French prophets and John Lacy. *The Psychoanalytic Review*, 1925, *12*, 16-29.

## 17. "PRIMITIVE" RELIGION.

Bidney, D. So-called primitive medicine and religion. In Gladston I. *Man's Image in Medicine and Anthropology.* New York: International Universities Press, 1963, 141-156.

Douglas, M. *Purity and Danger: An Analysis of Concepts of Pollution and Taboo.* London: Routledge & Kegan Paul, 1966, viii + 188 p.

Freeman, D. Thunder, blood and nicknaming God's creatures. *The Psychoanalytic Quarterly*, 1968, *37*, 353-399.

Kiev, A. Primitive religious rites and behaviour: clinical considerations. *International Psychiatry Clinics*, 1969, *5*, 119-131.

Kraus, R. F. A psychoanalytic interpretation of shamanism. *Psychoanalytic Review*, 1972, *59*, 19-32.

Roheim, G. *Australian Totemism: A Psycho-Analytic Study in Anthropology.* London: Allen & Unwin, 1925, 487 p.

Roheim, G. *Animism, Magic and the Divine King.* London: Kegan, Paul, Trench, Trubner: New York: Knopf, 1930, xviii + 390 p.

Roheim, G. Primitive high gods. *The Psychoanalytic Quarterly*, 1934, *3*, 1-133.

Roheim, G. The gods of primitive man and the religion of the Andamanesian pygmies. *The Psychoanalytic Review*, 1928, *15*, 105-106.

Roheim, G. Mythology of Arnhem Land. *American Imago*, 1951, *8*, 181-187.

Walsh, M. N. A psycoanalytic interpretation of a primitive dramatic ritual. *Journal of the Hillside Hospital*, 1962, *11*, 3-20.

Hopkins, P. Religious beliefs and practices in the land of the Incas. *Religions*, 1938.

## 18. GREEK RELIGION AND MYTHOLOGY.

Balter, L. The mother as a source of power: A psychoanalytic study of three Greek myths. *Psychoanalytic Quarterly*, 1969, *38*, 217-274.

Bunker, A. H. The feast of Tantalus. *Psychoanalytic Quarterly*, 1952, *21*, 355-372.

Bunker, A. H. Tantalus: A preoedipal figure of myth. *Psychoanalytic Quarterly*, 1953, *22*, 159-173.

Desmonde, W. H. The Eleusian mysteries. *Journal of the Hillside Hospital*, 1952, *1*, 204-218.

Desmonde W. H. The bull fight as a religious ritual. *American Imago*, 1952, *9*, 173-195.

Deutsch, H. *A Psychoanalytic Study of the Myth of Dionysus and Apollo.* New York: International Universities Press, 1969, 101 p.

Huckel, H. The tragic guilt of Prometheus. *American Imago*, 1955, *12*, 325-336.

Jacques, H. P. *Mythologie et Psychanalyse. Le Chatiment de Danaides.* (Mythology and Psychoanalysis. The Punishment of the Danaides.) Montreal: Les Editions Lemeac, 1969.

Lederer, W. Oedipus and the serpent. *The Psychoanalytic Review*, 1964-65, *51*, 619-644.

Lederer, W. Historical consequences of father-son hostility. *The Psychoanalytic Review*, 1967, *54*, 248-276.

Lidz, T. and Rothenberg, A. Psychedelism: Dyonysus reborn. *Psychiatry*, 1968, *31*, 116-125.

Lourie, A. The Jewish god and the Greek hero. *American Imago*, 1948, *5*, 152-166.

Marcus, N. N. Prometheus reconsidered. *Psychoanalytic Review*, 1967, *54*, 83-107.

Medlicott, R. W. Leda and the swan - An analysis of the theme in myth and art. *Australian and New Zealand Journal of Psychiatry*, 1970, *4*, 15-23.

Pearson, G. H. J. A note on the medusa: A speculative attempt to explain a ritual. *Bulletin of the Philadelphia Association for Psychoanalysis*, 1967, *17*, 1-9.

Schneck, J. M. Freud and Kronos. *American Journal of Psychaitry*, 1968, *125*, 692-693.

Schneiderman, L. A theory of repression in the light of archaic religion. *The Psychoanalytic Review*, 1966, *53*, 220-232.

Stokes, A. *Greek Culture and the Ego*. London: Tavistock, 1958, 101 p.

Ware, J. G. "Greater still is Diana of the Ephesians." *American Imago*, 1962, *19*, 253-275.

Wayne, R. Prometheus and Christ. *Psychoanalysis and the Social Sciences*, 1951, *3*, 201-219.

de Wolf, M. J. Comments on Freud and Kronos. *Psychoanalytic Quarterly*, 1972, *41*, 420-423.

See also section 8.

## 19. ISLAM.

El-Islam, M. F. The psychotherapeutic basis of some Arab rituals. *International Journal of Social Psychiatry*, 1967, *13*, 265-268.

## 20. JUDAISM - GENERAL.

Ackerman, N. W. and Jahoda, M. *Anti-Semitism and Emotional Disorder: A Psychoanalytic Interpretation.* New York: Harper, 1950.

Almansi, R. J. Ego-psychological implications of a religious symbol. A cultural and experimental study. *The Psychoanalytic Study of Society*, 1964, *3*, 39-70.

Bakan, D. *The Duality of Human Existence.* Chicago: Rand McNally, 1966.

Brenner, A. B. Some psychoanalytic speculations on Anti-semitism. *Psychoanalytic Review*, 1948, *35*, 20-32.

Brenner, A. B. The great mother goddess; puberty initiation rites and the covenant of Abraham. *Psychoanalytic Review*, 1950, *37*, 320-340.

Brenner, A. B. The covenant with Abraham. *The Psychoanalytic Review*, 1952, *39*, 34-52.

Brink, L. Frazer's *Folk Lore in the Old Testament.* A critical review. *The Psychoanalytic Review*, 1922, 9, 218-254.

Brody, M. Phylogenesis of sexual morality: Psychiatric exegesis on Onan and Samson. *New York State Journal of Medicine*, 1968, *68*, 2510-2512.

Chandler, T. Ikhnaton and Moses. *American Imago*, 1962, *19*, 127-139.

Cronbach, A. The psychoanalytic study of Judaism. *Hebrew Union College Annual*, 1931-32, *8-9*, 605-740.

Cronbach, A. New studies in the psychology of Judaism. *Hebrew Union College Annual*, 1946, *19*, 205-273.

Desmonde, W. H. The murder of Moses. *American Imago*, 1950, *7*, 351-367.

Feldman, A. A. Freud's *Moses and Monotheism* and the three stages of Israelitic religion. *Psychoanalytic Review*, 1944, *31*, 361-418.

Fenichel, O. Psychoanalysis of antisemitism. *American Imago*, 1940, *1*, 24-39.

Franzblau, A. N. Judaism and psychoanalysis. *Dimension*, 1967, *1*, 15-20, 30-31.

Gilbert, A. A rabbinic theory of instincts. *Psychoanalysis, Journal of the National Psychological Association for Psychoanalysis*, 1955, *3*, 36-43.

Glenn, J. Circumcision and anti-Semitism *Psychoanalytic Quarterly*, 1960, *29*, 395-399.

Goitein, L. The importance of the Book of Job for analytic thought. *American Imago*, 1954, *11*, 407-415.

Goitein, L. Green Pastures: Psalm xxiii. *American Imago*, 1956, *13*, 409-414.

Greenberger, B. The anti-Semite and the oedipal conflict. *International Journal of Psychoanalysis*, 1964, *45*, 380-385.

Grollman, E. A. Some sights and insights of history, psychology and psychoanalysis concerning the Father-god and Mother goddess concepts of Judaism and Christianity. *American Imago*, 1963, *20*, 187-209.

Howland, A. H. "Bosheth" or "Kadesh?" A study into the sources of the obscene ideas about obscenity. *Journal of Sexology and Psychoanalysis*, 1923, *1*, 289-296.

Jones, E. The psychology of the Jewish question. In Jones, E. *Essays in Applies Psycho-Analysis*. London, Vienna: International Psychoanalytic Press. London: The Hogarth Press and the Institute of Psycho-Analysis, 1951, *1*, 284-300.

Jones, E. The birth and death of Moses. *International Journal of Psychoanalysis*, 1958, *39*, 1-4.

Kaplan, L. The Baalschem Legend (Tr. Green, A.). *Psyche and Eros*, 1921, *2*, 173-183.

Krapf, E. E. Shylock and Antonia: A psychoanalytic study of Shakespeare and anti-semitism. *Psychoanalytic Review*, 1955, *42*, 113-130.

Lederer, W. Oedipus and the serpent. *The Psychoanalytic Review*, 1964-65, *51*, 619-644.

Lederer, W. Historical consequences of father-son hostility. *The Psychoanalytic Review*, 1967, *54*, 248-276.

Loeblowitz-Lennard, H. A psychoanalytic contribution to the problem of antisemitism. *Psychoanalytic Review*, 1945, *32*, 359-361.

Loeblowitz-Lennard, H. The Jew as symbol. I. The ritual murder myth. *Psychoanalytic Quarterly*, 1947, *16*, 33-38.

Loeblowitz-Lennard, H. The Jew as symbol. II. Anti-Semitism and transference. *Psychiatric Quarterly*, 1947, *21*. 253-260.

Lowenstein, R. M. The historical and cultural roots of anti-Semitism. In *Psychoanalysis and the Social Sciences*, 1947, *1*, 313-356.

Loewenstein, R. M. *Christians and Jews*. New York: International Universities Press, 1951.

Lorand, S. Dream interpretation in the Talmud. *International Journal of Psychoanalysis*, 1957, *38*, 92-97.

Lourie, A. The Jewish God and the Greek hero. *American Imago*, 1948, *5*, 152-166.

Lourie, A. The Jew as a psychological type. *American Imago*, 1949, *6*, 119-155.

Lustig, E. On the origins of Judaism: A psychoanalytic approach. *The Psychoanalytic Study of Society*, 1976, *7*, 359-367.

Natterson, J. M. Jewishness as resistance. *The Psychoanalytic Review*, 1966, *53*, 94-98,

Pederson, S. Unconscious motives in pro-semitic attitudes. *Psychoanalytic Review*, 1951, *38*, 361-373.

Peto, A. The demonic mother image in the Jewish religion. In Muensterberger, W. and Axelrad, S. *Psychoanalysis and the Social Sciences*. New York: International Universities Press, 1958, *5*, 280 - 287.

Peto, A. The development of ethical monotheism. *The Psychoanalytic Study of Society*, 1960, *1*, 311-375.

Ramnoux, C. Sur une page de "Moise et le monotheisme" (About a page from "Moses and monotheism"). *Psychanalyse*, 1957, *3*, 165-187.

Roheim, G. Some aspects of Semitic monotheism. *Psychoanalysis and the Social Sciences*, 1955, *4*, 169-222.

Rosenzweig, E. M. Some notes, historical and psychoanalytical on the people of Israel and the land of Israel with special reference to Deuteronomy. *American Imago*, 1940, *1*, 50-64.

Schick, A. The Jew as sacrificial victim. *Psychoanalytic Review*, 1971, *58*, 75-89.

Schlossman, H. God the father and his sons. *American Imago*, 1972, *8*, 35-51.

Schoenfeld, C. G. Psychoanalysis and anti-semitism. *The Psychoanalytic Review*, 1966, *53*, 24-37.

Schneiderman, L. Psychological evolution from polytheism to monotheism. *The Psychoanalytic Review*, 1964, *51*, 274-284.

Siegel, L. M. A bar to conversion. *The Psychoanalytic Review*, 1966, *53*, 16-23.

Sillman, L. R. Monotheism and the sense of reality. *International Journal of Psycho-Analysis*, 1949, *30*, 124-132.

## 21. JUDAISM - ARTIFACTS.

Almansi, R. J. A psychoanalytic interpretation of the Menorah. *Journal of the Hillside Hospital*, 1953, *2*, 80-95.

Almansi, R. J. A further contribution to the psychoanalytic interpretation of the Menorah. *Journal of the Hillside Hospital*, 1954, *3*, 3-18.

Eder, M. D. The Jewish phylacteries and other Jewish ritual observances. *International Journal of Psycho-Analysis*, 1933, *14*, 341-375.

Garma, A. The origin of clothes. *The Psychoanalytic Quarterly*, 1949, *18*, 173-190.

Palm, R. On the symbolic significance of the Star of David. *American Imago*, 1958, *15*, 227-231.

Reik, T. The Shofar (Ram's Horn). In Author's *Ritual: Psychoanalytic Studies*, 221-361.

Reik, T. The prayer shawl and phylacterics of the Jews: A psychoanalytic contribution to Hebrew archeology. In author's *Dogma and Compulsion: Psychoanalytic Studies of Myths and Religions*, 181-228.

## 22. JUDAISM - DOGMA.

Barag, G. The mother in the religious concepts of Judaism. *American Imago*, 1946, *4*, 32-53.

Barag, G. The question of Jewish monotheism. *American Imago*, 1947, *4*, 8-25.

Douglas, M. *Purity and Danger: An Analysis of Concepts of Pollution and Taboo.* London: Routledge & Kegan Paul, 1966, viii + 188 p.

Fodor, A. The origin of the Mosaic prohibition against cooking the suckling in its mother's milk. *International Journal of Psychoanalysis*, 1946, *27*, 140-144.

Fodor, N. A personal analytic approach to the problem of the Holy Name. *Psychoanalytic Review*, 1944, *31*, 165 - 180.

Reik, T. The face of God. *Psychoanalysis*, 1955, *3*, (2), 3-26.

Roheim, G. Some aspects of Semitic monotheism. *Psychoanalysis and the Social Sciences*, 1955, *4*, 169-222.

Schoenfeld, C. G. Psychoanalysis and anti-semitism. *The Psychoanalytic Review*, 1966, *53*, 24-37.

Woolf, M. Prohibitions against the simultaneous consumption of milk and flesh in orthodox Jewish laws. *International Journal of Psycho-Analysis*, 1945, *26*, 169-177.

## 23. JUDAISM - HOLIDAYS.

Beit-Hallahmi, B. Sacrifice, fire and the victory of the sun: A search for the origins of Hanukkah. *Psychoanalytic Review*, 1977, *63*, 497-509.

Reik, Theodor. A Booth away from the House. *Psychoanalytic Review*, 1963, *50*, 167-86.

Reik, T. *Pagan Rites in Judaism.* New York: Noonday Press, 1964.

Roheim, G. Some aspects of Semitic monotheism. *Psychoanalysis and the Social Sciences*, 1955, *4*, 169-222.

Schlesinger, K. Origins of the Passover Seder in ritual sacrifice. *The Psychoanalytic Study of Society*, 1976, *7*, 369-399.

## 24. JUDAISM - MYTHOLOGY.

Anderson, F. A. Psychopathological glimpses of some biblical characters. *The Psychoanalytic Review*, 1927, *14*, 56-70.

Arlow, J. A. The consecration of the prophet. *Psychoanalytic Quarterly*, 1951, *20*, 374-397.

Barag, G. The mother in the religious concepts of Judaism. *American Imago*, 1956, *4*, 32-53.

Barag, G. The question of Jewish monotheism. *American Imago*, 1947, *4*, 8-25.

Beck, S. J. Abraham's ordeal: Creation of a new reality. *Psychoanalytic Review*, 1963, *50*, 334-349.

Beck, S. J. Cosmic optimism in some Genesis myths. *American Journal of Orthopsychiatry*, 1971, *41*, 380-389.

Brenner, A. B. The great mother goddess: Puberty initiation rites and the covenant of Abraham. *The Psychoanalytic Review*, 1950, *37*, 320-340.

**Brenner, A. B. The covenant with Abraham.** *The Psychoanalytic Review*, 1952, *39*, 34-52.

**Brenner, A. B. Onan, the levirate marriage and the genealogy of the Messiah.** *Journal of the American Psychoanalytic Association*, 1962, *10*, 701-721.

Brody, M. Phylogenesis of sexual morality: Psychiatric exegesis on Onan and Samson. *New York State Journal of Medicine*, 1968, *68*, 2510-2512.

Feldman, A. A. The Davidic dynasty and the Davidic Messiah. *American Imago*, 1960, *17*, 163-178.

Feldman, S. S. The sin of Reuben, first-born son of Jacob. In W. Munsterberger & S. Axelrad (Eds.) *Psychoanalysis and the Social Sciences*. Vol. IV. New York: International Universities Press, 1955.

Fingert, H. H. Psychoanalytic study of the minor prophet, Jonah. *The Psychoanalytic Review*, 1954, *41*, 55-65.

Fodor, A. Was Moses an Egyptian? *Psychoanalysis and the Social Sciences*, 1951, *3*, 189.

Fodor, A. The fall of man in the book of Genesis. *American Imago*, 1954, *11*, 201-231.

Freehof, S. W. Three psychiatric stories from Rabbinic lore. *Psychoanalytic Review*, 1942, *29*, 185-187.

Fromm, E. *You Shall Be As Gods: A Radical Interpretation of the Old Testament and Its Tradition.* New York: Holt, Rinehart and Winston, 240 p.

Gonen, J. Y. Then men said, "Let us make God in our image after our likeness." *Literature and Psychology*, 1971, *21*, 69-79.

Graves, R. and Patai, R. Some Hebrew myths and legends. *Encounter*, 1963, *20*, 3-18; *20* (3), 12-18.

Katz, J. The Joseph dream anew. *Psychoanalytic Review*, 1963, *50*, 252-278.

Katz, R. L. A psychoanalytic comment on Job 3.25. *Hebrew Union College Annual*, 1958, *29*, 377-383.

Leschnitzer, A. F. Faust and Moses. *American Imago*, 1949, *6*, 229-243.

Levin, A. J. Oedipus and Samson, the rejected hero-child. *International Journal of Psychoanalysis*, 1957, *38*, 105-116.

de Monchy, S. J. R. Adam-Cain-Oedipus. *American Imago*, 1962, *19*, 3-17.

More, J. The prophet Jonah: The story of an intrapsychic process. *American Imago*, 1970, *27*, 3-11.

Naftalin, M. Footnote to the genesis of Moses. *The Psychoanalytic Quarterly*, 1958, *27*, 402-405.

Niederland, W. G. Jacob's dream: With some remarks on ladder and river symbolism. *Journal of the Hillside Hospital*, 1954, *3*, 73-97.

Oehschlegel, L. Regarding Freud's book on Moses: A religio-psychoanalytical study. *The Psychoanalytic Review*, 1943, *30*, 67-77.

Peto, A. The demonic mother image in the Jewish religion. *Psychoanalysis and the Social Sciences*, 1958, *5*, 280-287.

Reik, T. *Dogma and Compulsion: Psychoanalytic Studies of Religion and Myths.* New York: International Universities Press, 1951.

Reik, T. *Myth and Guilt.* New York: Braziller, 1957.

Reik, T. *Mystery of the Mountain: The Drama of the Sinai Revelation.* New York: Harper, 1959, xiii + 210 p.

Reik, T. *The Creation of Woman: A Psychoanalytic Inquiry into the Myth of Eve.* New York: G. Braziller 1960, viii + 159 p.

Reik, T. *The Temptation.* New York Braziller 1961, 256 p.

Reik, T. Psychoanalytic Studies of Bible Exegesis I. The wrestling of Jacob. In author's *Dogma and Compulsion: Psychoanalytic Studies of Myth and Religions*, 229-275.

Roheim, G. The covenant of Abraham. *The International Journal of Psycho-analysis,* 1939, *20*, 452-459.

Roheim, G. The Garden of Eden. *Psychoanalytic Review*, 1940, *27*, 1-26: 177-199.

Rosenfeld, E. M. The pan-headed Moses - A parallel. *International Journal of Psychoanalysis*, 1951, *32*, 83-93.

Rosenzweig, E. M. Some notes, historical and psychoanalytical, on the people of Israel and the land of Israel with special reference to Deuteronomy. *American Imago*, 1940, *1*, 50-64.

Rubenstein, R. L. The significance of castration anxiety in Rabbinic mythology. *The Psychoanalytic Review*, 1963, *50*, 289-312.

Rubenstein, R. L. *The Religious Imagination.* New York: Bobbs-Merrill, 1967, 256 p.

Segal, B. Serpent - staffs of antiquity. *Hebrew Medical Journal*, 1963, *2*, 229-231.

Seidenberg, R. Sacrificing the first you see. *The Psychoanalytic Review*, 1966, *53*, 49-62.

Slap, J. W. The Genesis of Moses. *Psychoanalytic Quarterly*, 1958, *27*, 400-402.

Slochower, H. The Book of Job: The Hebrew myth of the Chosen God, its symbolism and psychoanalytic process. *International Record of Medicine*, 1958, *171*, 761-769.

Teslaar, J. S. Van. The theogeny of "El" (A biblical instance of purposive condensation). *Psyche and Eros*, 1920, *1*, 114-117.

Theodoropoulus, J. "Adam's Rib." *The Psychoanalytic Review*, 1967, *54*, 150-152.

Wallace, E. R. The psychodynamic determinants of *Totem and Taboo*. *Psychiatry*, 1977, *40*, 79-87.

Weiss, S. A. The Biblical story of Ruth: Analytic implications of the Hebrew masoretic text. *American Imago*, 1959, *16*, 195-209.

Wellisch, E. *Isaac and Oedipus: A Study in Biblical Psychology of the Sacrifice of Isaac, the Akedah.* London: Routledge & Kegan Paul, 1954, 131 p.

Zeligs, D. F. Psychological factors in the teaching of Bible stories. *Jewish Education*, 1951, *22*, 24-28.

Zeligs, D. F. Two episodes in the life of Jacob. *American Imago*, 1953, *10*, 181 - 202.

Zeligs, D. Abraham and monotheism. *American Imago*, 1954, *11*, 293-316.

Zeligs, D. F. The personality of Joseph. *American Imago*, 1955, *12*, 47-69.

Zeligs, D. F. A character study of Samuel. *American Imago*, 1955, *12*, 355-386.

Zeligs, D. F. Saul, the tragic king. *American Imago*, 1957, *14*, 61-100.

Zeligs, D. F. A psychoanalytic note on the function of the Bible. *American Imago*, 1957, *14*, 57-60.

Zeligs, D. F. The mother in Hebraic Monotheism. *The Psycho-analytic Study of Society*, 1960, *1*, 287 - 311.

Zeligs, D. F. A study of King David. *American Imago*, 1960, *17*, 179-200.

Zeligs, D. F. Solomon: Man and myth. *Psychoanalysis and the Psychoanalytic Review*, 1961, *48*, 77-103, 91-110.

Zeligs, D. F. The family romance of Moses. I. The "personal myth." *American Imago*, 1966, *23*, 110-131.

Zeligs, D. F. Moses in Midian: The burning bush. *American Imago*, 1969, *26*, 379-400.

Zeligs, D. F. Moses and pharaoh: A psychoanalytic study of their encounter. *American Imago*, 1973, *30*, 192-220.

Zeligs, D. F. *Psychoanalysis and the Bible*, New York: Bloch Publishing Company, 1974.

See also section 27.

## 25. JUDAISM - RITUAL.

Arlow, J. A. A psychoanalytic study of a religious initiation rite. *The Psychoanalytic Study of the Child*, 1951, *6*, 353-374.

Daly, C. D. The psycho-biological origins of circumcision. *International Journal of Psychoanalysis*, 1950, *31*, 217-236.

Eder, M. D. The Jewish phylacteries and other Jewish ritual observances. *International Journal of Psycho-Analysis*, 1933, *14*, 341-375.

Feldman, S. S. The blessing of the Kohenites. *American Imago*, 1941, *2*, 296-322.

Feldman, S. S. Notes on some religious rites and ceremonies. *Journal of the Hillside Hospital*, 1959, *8*, 36-41.

Fraenkel, E. La circoncision chez les Juifs peut-elle s'expliquer comme une castration attenuee, infliquee a ses fils par le chef de la horde. *Psyche*, 1952, *7*, 377-385.

Grinberg, L. Psychoanalytic considerations on the Jewish Passover: Totemic sacrifice and meal. *American Imago*, 1962, *19*, 391-424.

Maler, M. The Jewish Orthodox circumcision ceremony: Its meaning from direct study of the rite. *Journal of the American Psychoanalytic Association*, 1966, *14*, 510-517.

Nunberg, H. *Problems of bisexuality as reflected in circumcision*, Lndon: Imago Publishing, 1949,

Reik, T. *Dogma und Compulsion*. New York: International Universities Press, 1951.

Reik, T. A booth away from the house. *The Psychoanalytic Review*, 1963, *50*, 167-186.

Reik, T. *Pagan Rites in Judaism*, New York: Farrar, Straus, 1964, 206 p.

Schlesinger, K. Origins of the Passover Seder in ritual sacrifice. *The Psychoanalytic Study of Society*, 1976, *7*, 369-399.

Schlossman, H. H. Circumcision as defense: A study in psycho-analysis and religion. *The Psychoanalytic Quarterly*, 1966, *35*, 340-356.

Zimmermann, F. Origin and significance of the Jewish rite of circumcision. *Psychoanalytic Review*, 1951, *38*, 103-112.

## 26. FREUD, JUDAISM AND PSYCHOANALYSIS.

Amsel, A. *Judaism and Psychology.* New York: Philipp Feldheim, 1969, xv + 213 p.

Aron, W. Freudiana Judaica. *Jewish Forum* (N. Y.), 1956, June 98-99, August 104-105, September 138-139.

Bakan, D. Freud's Jewishness and his psychoanalysis. *Judaism*, 1954, *3*, (1) 20-26.

Bakan, D. *Sigmund Freud and the Jewish Mystical Tradition.* Princeton, New Jersey: Van Nostrand, 1958, xix + 326 p.

Baruk, H. La signification de la psychanalyse et le judaisme (The significance of psychoanalysis and Judaism). *Rev. Hist. med. hebr.*, 1966, *19*, 15-29, 53-65; 131-132.

Berkower, L. The enduring effect of the Jewish tradition upon Freud. *American Journal of Psychiatry, 125,* 1067-1075.

Freud. S. Preface to the Hebrew translation of Totem and Taboo (1934). In *The Complete Psychological Works of Sigmund Freud.* London: The Hogart Press, 1955, *13*, XV.

Freud, S. Letter to the director of Judische Presszentrale Zurich (1925). In Strachey, J. (Ed.) *Standard Edition of the Complete Psychological Works of Sigmund Freud.* London: The Hogarth Press and the Institute of Psycho-Analysis, *19*, 1961, p. 291.

Freud, S. An autobiographical study (1925). In *The Complete Psychological Works of Sigmund Freud.* London: Hogarth Press, 1959, *20*, 1-74.

Freud, S. On the occasion of the opening of the Hebrew University (1925). In *The Standard Edition of the Complete Psychological Works of Sigmund Freud.* London: The Hogarth Press, 1961, *19*, 292.

Freud, S. Address to members of the B'nai B'rith (1926). In Strachey, J. (Ed.) *Standard Edition of the Complete Psychological Works of Sigmund Freud.* London: The Hogarth Press and the Institute of Psycho-Analysis, *20*, 271-276.

Freud, S. *The Letters of Sigmund Freud* (Ed. Freud, E. L.) (Tr. Stern, T. and Stern, J. ). New York: Basic Books, 1960, viii + 470 p.

Grollman, E. A. *Judaism in Sigmund Freud's World* (Foreword: Ackerman, N. W.). New York: Block Publishing Company, 1966, xxv + 173 p.

Lewis, T. N. Freud, the Jew and Judaism. *Jewish Spectator*. New York: 1958, March 11-14.

Loewenberg, P. Sigmund Freud as a Jew: A study in ambivalence and courage. *Journal of the History of the Behavioral Sciences*, 1972, 7, 363-369.

Lublin, M. Study of the high rate of male Jewish membership in the profession of psychoanalysis. *Proceedings of the 77th Annual Convention of the American Psychological Association*, 1969, 4, 527-528.

Meadow, A. and Vetter, H. J. Freudian theory and the Judaic value system. *International Journal of Social Psychiatry*, 1959, 5, 197-207.

Menninger, K. A. The genius of the Jew in psychiatry. *Medical Leaves*, 1937, 1, 127-132.

Oehschlegel, L. Regarding Freud's book on Moses: A religio-psychoanalytical study. *The Psychoanalytic Review*, 1943, 30, 67-77.

Reik, T. Freud and Jewish wit. *Psychoanalysis, Journal of the National Psychological Association for Psychoanalysis*, 1954, 2, 12-20.

Roback, A. A. Freudian psychology and Jewish commentators of the Bible. *Jewish Forum*. 1918, 1, 528-533.

Roback, A. A. Is psychoanalysis a Jewish movement? *B'nai B.rith Mag.*, 1926, 40, 118-119, 129-130, 198-201, 238-239.

Robert, M. *From Oedipus to Moses*. Garden City, New York: Doubleday, 1977.

Rubenstein, R. L. Freud and Judaism: A review article. *Journal of Religion*, 1967, 47, 39-44.

Steinletz, E. Hassidism and psychoanalysis. *Judaism*, 1960, 9, 222-229.

Wallace, E. R. The psychodynamic determinants of *Totem and Taboo*. *Psychiatry*, 1977, *40*, 79-87.

Wolff, W. Freud the Jew. *Jewish Spectator*, New York, (May) 1958, 27.

See also 3, 4, 5.

# 27. MYTHOLOGY - GENERAL AND COMPARATIVE.

Abou, Z. La psychanalyse des mythes. *Egyptian Journal of Psychology*, 1946, *2*, 233-251.

Abraham, K. Dreams and myths (1909). In K. Abraham *Clinical Papers and Essays on Psychoanalysis*. New York: Basic Books, 1955.

Arlow, J. A. Ego psychology and the study of mythology. *Journal of the American Psychoanalytic Association*, 1961, *9*, 371-393.

Arlow, J. A. The Madonna's conception through the ear. *The Psychoanalytic Study of Society*, 1964, *3*, 13-25.

Barnouw, V. A psychological interpretation of a Chippewa origin legend. *Journal of American Folklore*, 1955, *68*, 73-85, 211-223, 341-355.

Badouin, C. *Psychanalyse de Symbole Religieuse*. Parix: Fayard, 1957.

Beit-Hallahmi, B. and Paluszny, M. Twinship in mythology and science: Ambivalence, differentiation, and the magical bond. *Comprehensive Psychiatry*, 1974, *15*, 345-353.

Bellah, R. N. Father and son in Christianity and Confusianism. *The Psychoanalytic Review*, 1965, *52*, 92-114.

Bergmann, M. S. The impact of ego psychology on the study of myth. *American Imago*, 1966, *23*, 257-264.

Bonaparte, M. Universal myths. In Lorand, S. (Ed.) *The Yearbook of Psychoanalysis*. New York: International Universities Press, 1946.

Boyer, L. B. and Boyer, R. M. A combined anthropological and psychoanalytic contribution to folklore. *Psychopathologie Africaine*, 1967, *3*, 333-372.

Campbell, J. *The Hero with a Thousand Faces*. New York: Pantheon Books, 1949, xxiii + 416 p.

Campbell, J. Bios and Mythos: Prolegomena to a science of mythology. In Wilbur, G. and Muensterberger, W. (Eds.)

*Psychoanalysis and Culture*. New York: International Universities Press, 1961.

Campbell, J. *The Masks of God: Primitive Mythology*. New York: Viking, 1959, 504 p.

Campbell, J. Ed. *Man and Transformation* (Tr: Manheim, R.) New York: Pantehon Books, 1964, xviii + 413 p.

Campbell, J. (Ed.) *Myths Dreams, and Religion*. New York: E. P. Dutton & Co., 1970, 355 p.

Campbell, J. *The Flight of the Garden: Explorations in the Mythological Dimension*, 2nd Ed. Chicago: Henry Regenry Co., 1972, 248 p.

de Cavalho-Netto, P. *Folklore and Psychoanalysis*. Coral Gables, Fla.; University of Miami Press, 1972.

Cologeras, R. C. Levi-Strauss and Freud: Their 'structural' approaches to myth. *American Imago*, 1973, *30*, 57-79.

Cox, H. L. The place of mythology in the study of culture. *American Imago*, 1948, *5*, 83-94.

Dorson, R. M. Theories of myth and the folklorist. *Daedalus*, 1959, *88*, 280-290.

Edelheit, H. Mythopoesis and the primal scene. *Psychoanalytic Study of Society*, 1972, *5*, 212-233.

Eliade, M. *Myths, Dreams and Mysteries*. New York: Harper, 1960.

Eliade, M. *Myth and Reality*. New York: Harper, 1963.

Freund, K. *Myths of Creation*. New York: Wash. Square Pr. 1965, vi + 304 p.

Freund, K. The meaning of myth to modern man. *Journal of the Otto Rank Association*, 1967, *2*, 52-53.

Fromm, E. *The Forgotten Language: An introduction to the understanding of dreams, fairy tales and myths*. New York: Rinehart, 1951, vii + 263 p.

Gedo, J. E. Mythopoesis and psychoanalysis. *American Imago*, 1970, *27*, 329-337.

Grinstein, A. Stages in the development of control over fire. *International Journal of Psycho-Analysis*, 1952, *33*, 416-420.

Grotjahn, M. *The Voice of the Symbol*. Los Angeles: Mara Books, 1971, xv + 224 p.

Hacker, F. J. The reality of myth. *International Journal of Psychoanalysis*, 1964, *45*, 438-443.

Hyman, S. E. The ritual view of myth and mythic. In J. B. Vickery (Ed.) *Myth and Literature: Contemporary theory and practice*. Lincoln: University of Nebraska Press, 1966.

Jones, E. *Nightmares, Witches and Devils*. New York: Norton, 1931.

Kaplan, B. Psychological themes in Zuni mythology and Zuni TAT's. *The Psychoanalytic Study of Society*, 1962, *2*, 255-262.

Karlson, K. J. Psychoanalysis and mythology. *Journal of Religious Psychology*, 1914, *7*, 137-213.

Kluckhohn, C. Myths and rituals: A general theory. *Harvard Theological Review*, 1942, *35*, 45-79.

Kluckhohn, C. Recurrent themes in myths and myth-making. *Daedalus*, 1959, *88*, 268-279.

Leach, E. R. (Ed.) *The Structural Study of Myth and Totemism*. London: Tavistock, 1967, 185 p.

Levin, A. J. Oedipus and Samson, the rejected hero-child. *International Journal of Psycho-Analysis*, 1957, *38*, 105-116.

Moloney, J. C. Carnal myths involving the sun. *American Imago*, 1963, *20*, 93-104.

Muensterberger, W. Remarks on the function of mythology. *The Psychoanalytic Study of Society*, 1964, *3*, 94-97.

Murray, H. A. (Ed.) *Myth and Mythmaking*. New York: Braziller, 1960, 381 p.

Neu, J. Genetic explanation in Totem and Taboo. In R. Wolheim (Ed.) *Freud*. Garden City, New York: Doubleday, 1974.

Panel. Mythology and ego psychology. *The Psychoanalytic Study of Society*, 1964, *3*, 4-87.

Rank, O. *The Myth of the Birth of the Hero; a Psychological Interpretation of Mythology.* Nervous and Mental Diseases Monograph Series 18, New York: Nervous and Mental Diseases Publishing Co., 1914, iii + 100 p.

Reik, T. Mythology (Collected Reviews) *International Journal of Psycho-Analysis*, 1921, *2*, 101-105.

Reik, T. Man the mythmaker. In T. Reik, *Dogma and Compulsion.* New York: International Universities Press, 1951.

Riklin, F. *Wishfulfillment and Symbolism in Fairy Tales.* New York: Nervous and Mental Diseases Publishing Company, 1915.

Roheim, G. *The Riddle of the Sphinx.* London: The Hogarth Press, 1934.

Roheim, G. Myth and folk tale. *American Imago*, 1941, *2*, 266-279.

Roheim, G. Aphrodite, or the woman with a penis. *Psychoanalytic Quarterly*, 1945, *14*, 350-390.

Roheim, G. The panic of the gods. *The Psychoanalytic Quarterly*, 1952, *21*, 92-106.

Slochower, H. Psychoanalytic distinction between myth and mythopoesis. *Journal of the American Psychoanalytic Association*, 1970, *18*, 150-164.

Slochower, H. *Mythopoesis*, Detroit: Wayne State University Press, 1970.

Spiro, M. E. and D' Andrade, R. G. A cross-cultural study of some supernatural beliefs. *American Anthropologist*, 1960, *60*, 456-466.

Spiro, M. E. Religious systems as culturally constituted defense mechanisms. In author's *Context and Meaning in Cultural Anthropology.* New York: Free Press, 1965, 100-113.

Stern, M. M. Ego psychology, myth and rite: Remarks about the relationship of the individual and the group. In Muensterberger, W. and Axelrad, S. (Eds.) *The Psychoanalytic Study of Society.* New York: International Universities Press, 1964, *3*, 71-93.

Tarachow, S. Mythology and ego psychology. *The Psychoanalytic Study of Society*, 1964, *3*, 9-12.

Tarachow, S. Ambiguity and human imperfection. *Journal of the American Psychoanalytic Association*, 1965, *13*, 85-101.

Watson, G. A psychologist's view of religious symbols. In Johnson, F. E. *Religious Symbolism*. New York: Institute for Religious and Social Studies, Harper, 1955, 117-127.

Wittels, F. Psychoanalysis and history: The Nibelungs and the Bible. *The Psychoanalytic Quarterly*, 1946, *15*, 88-103.

Zeckel, A. The totemistic significance of the unicorn. In Wilbur, G. and Muensterberger, W. (Eds.) *Psychoanalysis and Culture*. New York: International Universities Press, 1951, 344-360.

See also sections 14, 18 and 24.

## 28. ORIGINS OF RELIGION.

Argyle, M. and Beit-Hallahmi, B. *The Social Psychology of Religion.* London: Routledge & Kegan Paul, 1975 (Ch. 11).

Barande, R. La "pulsion de mort" comme nontransgression: survie et transfiguration du tabou de l'inceste (The "death-drive" as nontransgression: survival and transfiguration of the incest taboo). *Revue Francaise de Psychanalyse*, 1968, *32*, 465-502.

Barnes, F. F. The myth of the seal ancestors. *The Psychoanalytic Review*, 1953, *40*, 156-157.

Becker, E. A note on Freud's primal horde theory. *Psychoanalytic Quarterly*, 1961, *30*, 412-419.

Beit-Hallahmi, B. and Argyle, M. God as a father projection: The theory and the evidence. *British Journal of Medical Psychology*, 1975, *48*, 71-75.

Beres, D. Psychoanalytic notes on the history of morality. *Journal of the American Psychoanalytic Assocaition*, 1965, *13*, 337.

Bradley, N. Primal scene experience in human evolution and its phantasy derivatives in art, proto-science and philosophy. *The Psychoanalytic Study of Society*, 1967, *4*, 34-79.

Brill, A. A. Thoughts on life and death, on Vidonian All Soul's eve. *Psychiatric Quarterly*, 1947, *21*, 199-211.

Bunker, H. A. The Bouphonia, or ox-murder: A footnote to *Totem and Taboo*. *Psychoanalysis and the Social Sciences*, 1947, *1*, 165-169.

Bychowski, G. The ego and the introjects: Origin of religious experience. *Psychoanalysis and the Social Sciences*, 1958, *5*, 246-279.

Casey, R. P. Oedipus motivation in religious thought and fantasy. *Psychiatry*, 1942, *5*, 219-228.

Chasseguet-Smirgel, J. Oedipe et religion (Oedipus and religion). *Revue Francaise de Psychanalyse*, 1967, *31*, 875-882.

Dalmau, C. J. Anthropocentric aspects of religion. *The Psychoanalytic Review*, 1967, *54*, 679-687.

Desmonde, W. H. The eternal fire as a symbol of the state. *Journal of the Hillside Hospital*, 1953, *2*, 143-147.

Feldman, A. B. The word in the beginning. *The Psychoanalytic Review*, 1964, *51*, 79-98.

Feldman, S. Notes on the primal horde. *Psychoanalysis and the Social Sciences*, 1947, *1*, 171-194.

Ferenczi, S. Obsessional neurosis and piety. In *Further Contributions to Psychoanalysis*. London: Hogart Press, 1926.

Flugel, J. C. *Man, Morals and Society*. New York: International Universities Press, 1945.

Fox, R. *Totem and Taboo* reconsidered. In E. R. Leach (Ed.) *The Structural Study of Myth and Totemism*. London: Tavistock, 1967.

Freeman, D. Totem and Taboo: A reappraisal. *The Psychoanalytic Study of Society*, 1965, *4*, 9-33.

Fromm, E. Faith as a character trait. *Psychiatry*, 1942, *5*, 307-319.

Jacobs, L. I. The primal crime. *Psychoanalytic Review*, 1965, *52*, 456-484.

Jones, E. The inception of *Totem and Taboo*. *International Journal of Psychoanalysis*, 1956, *37*, 34-35.

Klauber, J. Notes on the psychical roots of religion, with particular reference to the development of Western Christianity. *International Journal of Psycho-analysis*, 1974, *55*, 249-255.

Kroeber, A. L. Totem and Taboo. *American Anthropologist*, 1920, *22*, 48-55.

Kroeber, A. L. "Totem and Taboo" in retrospect. *American Journal of Sociology*, 1939, *45*, 446-451.

La Barre, W. *The Ghost Dance: The Origins of Religion*. New York: Doubleday, 1970.

Malev, M. Discussion of the paper by John Klauber on "Psychical roots of religion." *International Journal of Psychoanalysis*, 1974, *55*, 257-259.

McLeish, J. Psychoanalytic imperialism: Freudian methodology and primitive religion. *Dublin Review*, 1960, *234*, 227-238.

de Monchy, S. J. R. Adam-Cain-Oedipus. *American Imago*, 1962, *19*, 3-17.

Muensterberger, W. (Ed.) *Man and His Cutlure: Psychoanalytic Anthropology After "Totem and Taboo."* New York: Toplinger Publishing Company, 1970.

Reiser, O. L. The biological origins of religion. *The Psychoanalytic Review*, 1932, *19*, 1-22.

Rizzuto, A. M. Object relations and the formation of the image of God. *British Journal of Medical Psychology*, 1974, *47*, 83-99.

Roheim, G. Dying gods and puberty ceremonies. *Journal of the Royal Anthropological Institute*. 1929, *59*, 181-197.

Roheim, G. *Animism, Magic and the Divine King.* New York: Knopf, 1930, xviii + 390 p.

Roheim, G. Animism and religion. *The Psychoanalytic Quarterly*, 1932, *1*, 59-112.

Roheim, G. Primitive high gods. *The Psychoanalytic Quarterly*, 1934, *3*, 1-133.

Roheim, G. *Psychoanalysis and Anthropology.* New York: International Universities Press, 1950.

Roheim G. The Oedipus complex, magic and culture. *Psychoanalysis and the Social Sciences*, 1950, *2*, 173-228.

Roheim, G. *The Origin and Function of Culture.* Garden City, New York: Doubleday, 1971, 146 p.

Schlossman, H. God the father and his sons. *American Imago*, 1972, *8*, 35-51.

Schmidberg, W. Original sin. *Psychoanalytic Review*, 1950, *37*, 140-142.

Schneiderman, L. A theory of repression in the light of archaic religion. *The Psychoanalytic Review*, 1966, *53*, 220-232.

Schoenfeld, C. G. God the father and mother: Study and extension of Freud's conception of God as an exalted father. *American Imago*, 1962, *19*, 213-324.

Schroeder, T. A contribution to the psychology of theism, the French prophets and John Lacy. *The Psychoanalytic Review*, 1925, *12*, 16-29.

Schroeder, T. Guilt and inferiority as creator of religious experience. *Psychoanalytic Review*, 1929, *16*, 46-54.

Smith, G. E. Freud's speculations in ethnology. *Monist*, 1923, *33*, 81-97.

Spitz, R. A. The genesis of magical and transcendent cults. *American Imago*, 1973, *29*, 1-10.

Thouless, R. H. A difference between religion and neurosis. In Strunk, O., Jr. (Ed.) *Readings in the Psychology of Religion*. Nashville, Tennessee: Abingdon Press, 1959, 228 p. From author's An Introduction to the Psychology of Religion. London: Cambridge University Press, 277-278.

Trevett, L. D. Origin of the creation myth: A hypothesis. *Journal of the American Psychoanalytic Association*, 1957, *5*, 461-468.

Veszy-Wagner, I. An Irish legend as proof of Freud's theory of joint parricide. *International Journal of Psychoanalysis*, 1957, *38*, 117-120.

Vollmerhausen, J. W. Religion, perfectionism and the fair deal. *American Journal of Psychoanalysis*, 1965, *25*, 203-215.

Wilbur, G. B. Soul belief and psychology. *The Psychoanalytic Review*, 1932, *19*, 319-326.

See also section 32.

## 29. PREHISTORICAL RELIGIONS.

Desmonde, W. H. The bull fight as a religious ritual. *American Imago*, 1952, *9*, 173-195.

Desmonde, W. H. The eternal fire as a symbol of the state. *Journal of the Hillside Hospital*, 1953, *2*, 143-147.

Kohen, M. The Venus of Willendorf. *American Imago*, 1946, *3*, 49-60.

Pearson, G. H. J. A note on the medusa: A speculative attempt to explain a ritual. *Bulletin of the Philadelphia Association for Psychoanalysis*, 1967, *17*, 1-9.

Suttie, I. D. Religion, racial character and mental and social health. *British Journal of Medical Psychology*, 1932, *12*, 289-314.

Troisiers, J. Menhirs, trilithons and dolmens: Their symbolism. *British Journal of Medical Psychology*, 1932, *12*, 337-342.

## 30. RELIGION, PERSONALITY, AND PSYCHOPATHOLOGY.

Arlow, J. A. The Madonna's conception through the eyes. *The Psychoanalytic Study of Society*, 1964, *3*, 13-25.

Bakan, D. Some thoughts on reading Augustine's "Confessions." *Journal for the Scientific Study of Religion*, 1965, *5*, 149-152.

Balint, M. *Problems of Human Pleasure and Behavior.* New York: Liveright, 1957.

Baudouin, C. La sublimation des images chex Huysmans lors de sa conversion. (Sublimation of images in Huysmans at the time of his religious conversion). *Psyche* - (Paris), 1950, *5*, 378-385.

Block, S. L. St. Augustine: On grief and other psychological matters. *American Journal of Psychiatry*, 1966, *122*, 943-946.

Cafferata, R. F. , S. J. L'influence du surmoi dans la formation religieuse. (The influence of the super-ego in the molding of religious feeling). *Psyche- Paris*, 1949, *4*, 413-422.

Charny, E. J. The confessions of St. Augustine. *Psychiatric Communications*, 1958, *1*, 101-111.

Cohen, S. B. The ontogenesis of prophetic behavior: A study in creative conscience formation. *Psychoanalysis and the Psychoanalytic Review*, 1962, *49*, 100-122.

Colm, H. N. Religious symbolism in child analysis. *Psychoanalysis, Journal of the National Psychological Association for Psychoanalysis*, 1953, *2*, 39-56.

Cronin, H. J. Psychoanalytic sources of religious conflicts. *Medical Record*, 1934, *139*, 32-34.

Duff, I. F. G. A psychoanalytical study of a phantasy of St. Thesese de l'enfant Jesus. *British Journal of Medical Psychology*, 1925, *5*, 345-357.

Eisler, E. R. The religious factor in mental disorder. *Journal of Abnormal Psychology*, 1924-25, *19*, 85-95.

Erikson, E. H. *Young Man Luther, A Study in Psychoanalysis and History*. New York: W. W. Norton, 1958, 288 p.

Evans, W. N. Notes on the conversion of John Bunyan: A study in English Puritanism. *International Journal of Psychoanalysis*, 1943, *24*, 176-185.

Fairbairn, W. R. D. Notes on the religious fantasies of a female patient. In *An Object-Relations Theory of the Personality*. New York: Basic Books, 1954, pp. 183-196.

Fodor, N. Jung's sermons to the dead. *The Psychoanalytic Review*, 1964, *51*, 74-78.

Fox, A. N. Post-homicidal contrition and religious conversion. *Psychiatric Quarterly*, 1943, *17*, 565-578.

Glueck, B. The God man or Jehovah complex. *New York Medical Journal*, 1915, *102*, 496-499.

Goodich, M. Childhood and adolescence among thirteenth century saints. *History of Childhood Quarterly*, 1973, *1*, 285-309.

Gordon, K. H., Jr. Religious prejudices in an eight-year-old boy. *The Psychoanalytic Quarterly*, 1965, *34*, 102-107.

Greenacre, P. A study on the nature of inspiration. I. Some special considerations regarding the phallic phase. *Journal of the American Psychoanalytic Association*, 1964, *12*, 6-31.

Guntrip, H. J. S. *Personality Structure and Human Interaction*. New York: International Universities Press, 1961.

Hitschmann, E. New varieties of religious experience: From William James to Sigmund Freud. In G. Roheim (Ed.) *Psychoanalysis and the Social Sciences*. New York: International Universities Press, 1947.

Hitschmann, E. Swedenborg's paranoia. *American Imago*, 1949, *6*, 45-50.

Jones, E. The God-complex. The belief that one is God and the resulting character traits. In Jones, E. *Essays in Applied*

*Psycho-Analysis*. London: Vienna: International Psychoanalytic Press, 1923, 204-226. London: The Hogarth Press and the Institute of Psycho-Analysis, 1951, *2*, 244-265.

Kamiat, A. H. A psychology of asceticism. *Journal of Abnormal and Social Psychology*, 1928, *23*, 223-232.

Kaufman, M. R. Religious delusions in schizophrenia. *International Journal of Psycho-Analysis*, 1939, *20*, 363-376.

Klein, M. *Contributions to Psychoanalysis, 1921-1945*. London: Hogarth Press, 1965.

Kligerman, C. A psychoanalytic study of the confessions of St. Augustine. *Journal of the American Psychoanalytic Association*, 1957, *5*, 469-484.

Knight, R. P. Practical and theoretical considerations in the analysis of a minister. *Psychoanalytic Review*, 1937, *24*, 350-364.

Levin, T. M. and Zegans, L. S. Adolescent identity crisis and religious conversion: Implications for psychotherapy. *British Journal of Medical Psychology*, 1974, *47*, 73-82.

Lombillo, J. R. The soldier saint - a psychological analysis of the conversion of Ignatius of Loyola. *Psychiatric Quarterly*, 1973, *47*, 386 - 418.

Lowtzky, F. Soeren Kierkegaard: l'experience subjective et la revelation religieuse. Etude psychanalytique. *Revue Francaise de Psychanalyse*, 1936, *9*, 204-315.

Lubin, A. J. A feminine Moses: A bridge between childhood idendifications and adult identity. *International Journal of Psychoanalysis*, 1958, *39*, 535-546.

Lubin, A. J. The influence of the Russian Orthodox Church on Freud's Wolf - Man: a hypothesis (with an epilogue based on visits with the Wolf-Man). *The Psychoanalytic Forum*, 1967, *2*, 146-162, 170-174, 284-285.

Medlicott, R. W. St. Anthony Abbot and the hazards of asceticism: An analysis of artists' representations of the temptations. *British Journal of Medical Psychology*, 1969, *42*, 133-140.

Mora, G. The scrupulosity syndrome. *International Psychiatric Clinics*, 1969, *5*, 163-174.

Moxon, C. Epileptic traits in Paul of Tarsus. *Psychoanalytic Review*, 1922, *9*, 60-66.

Novey, S. Considerations on religion in relation to psychoanalysis and psychotherapy. *Journal of Nervous and Mental Diseases*, 1960, *130*, 315-324.

Rosenzweig, E. M. Minister and congregation - a study in ambivalence. *Psychoanalytic Review*, 1941, *28*, 218-227.

Rubin, J. L. Neurotic attitudes toward religion. *American Journal of Psychoanalysis*, 1955, *15*, 71-81.

Saffady, W. The effects of childhood bereavement and parental remarriage in sixteenth century England: The case of Thomas More. *History of Childhood Quarterly*, 1973, *1*, 310-336.

Schroeder, T. A "living God" incarnate. *Psychoanalytic Review*, 1932, *19*, 36-46.

Sessions, P. M. Ego religion and superego religion in alcoholics. *Quarterly Journal of Studies on Alcohol*, 1957, *18*, 121-125.

Smith, P. Luther's early development in the light of psychoanalysis. *American Journal of Psychology*, 1913, *24*, 360-377.

Thrift, I. E. Religion and madness. The case of William Cowper. *Psychoanalytic Review*, 1926, *13*, 312-317.

Weisner, W. M. and Riffel, R. P. A. Scrupulosity: Religion and obsessive compulsive behavior in children. *American Journal of Psychiatry*, 1960, *117*, 314-318.

Woolcott, P. Some considerations of creativity and religious experience in St. Augustine of Hippo. *Journal for the Scientific Study of Religion*, 1966, *5*, 273-283.

See also section 31.

## 31. RELIGIOUS THINKING AND RELIGIOUS EXPERIENCE.

Allison, J. Adaptive regression and intense religious experiences. *Journal of Nervous and Mental Diseases*, 1967, *145*, 452-463.

Allison, J. Religious conversion: regression and progression in an adolescent experience. *Journal for the Scientific Study of Religion*, 1969, *8*, 23-38.

Benassy, M. Psychanalyses didactiques et experiences religieuses (Training psychoanalyses and religious experiences). *Revue Franciase de Psychanalyse*, 1965, *29*, 31-41.

Bergman, P. A religious conversion in the course of psychotherapy. *American Journal of Psychotherapy*, 1953, *7*, 41-58.

Bjerre, P. C. The way to grace. *The Psychoanalytic Review*, 1927, *14*, 255-267.

Cohen, S. B. The ontogenesis of prophetic behavior: A study in creative conscience formation. *Psychoanalysis and the Psychoanalytic Review*, 1962, *49*, 100-122.

Darlington, H. S. The confession of sins. *Psychoanalytic Review*, 1937, *24*, 150-164.

Deikman, A. J. De-automatization and the mystic experience. *Psychiatry*, 1966, *24*, 324-338.

Devereux, G. Belief, superstition, and symptom. *Samiksa*, 1954, *8*, 210-215.

Eisenbud, J. Negative reactions to Christmas. *Psychoanalytic Quarterly*, 1941, *10*, 639-645.

Ekstein, R. A clinical note on the therapeutic use of a quasi-religious experience. *Journal of the American Psychoanalytic Association*, 1956, *4*, 304-313.

Feiner, A. H. and Levenson, E. A. The compassionate sacrifice: An explanation of a metaphor. *The Psychoanalytic Review*, 1968-69, *55*, 552-573.

Fisher, D. J. Sigmund Freud and Romain Rolland: The terrestrial animal and his great oceanic friend. *American Imago*, 1976, *33*, 1-59.

Franzblau, A. N. Conversion, psychologically speaking. In Eichhorn, D. M. *Conversion to Judaism: A history and analysis*. New York: Ktav Publishers, 1965, 189-207.

Fromm, E. Faith, as a character trait. *Psychiatry*, 1942, *5*, 307-319.

Gordon, R. *Stereotype of Imagery and Belief as a Ego Defense*. New York: Cambridge Univ. Pr., 1962, vii + 96 p.

Isaacs, K. S., Alexander, J. M. and Haggard, E. A. Faith, trust and gullibility. *International Journal of Psychoanalysis*, 1963, *44*, 461-469.

Kamiat, A. H. Further remarks on the believer's delusion of infallibility. *Psychoanalytic Review*, 1926, *13*, 304-311.

Kupper, H. I. Psychodynamics of the intellectual. *International Journal of Psycho-Analysis*, 1949, *30*, 201-202: 1950, *31*, 85-94.

Laforgue, R. La pensee magique dans la religion (Magic thought in religion). *Revue Francaise de Psychanalyse*, 1934, 7, 19-31.

Leavy, S. A. A religious conversion in a four-year-old girl: A historical note. *Bulletin of the Philadelphia Association for Psychoanalysis*, 1957, 7, 85-90.

Lehrman, S. R. Psychopathology in mixed marriages. *The Psychoanalytic Quarterly*, 1967, *36*, 67-82.

Lorand, S. Psycho-analytic therapy of religious devotees (A theoretical and technical contribution). *The International Journal of Psycho-Analysis*, 1962, *43*, 50-56.

Lubin, A. J. A boy's view of Jesus. In R. S. Eissler et al. (Eds.) *The Psychoanalytic Study of the Child*, 1959, *3*, 155-168.

McClelland, D. C. *Psychoanalysis and Religious Mysticism*. Wallingford, Pa.: Pendle Hill, 1959, 32 p.

Milner, M. The sense in non-sense (Freud and Blake's "Job"). *New Era*, London, 1956, *7*, 29-41.

Misch, R. C. Impulse control and social feeling. *International Psychiatry Clinics*, 1966, *3*, 117-137.

Moller, H. Affective mysticism in Western civilization. *The Psychoanalytic Review*, 1965, *52*, 259-274.

Oyama, J. Psycho-analysis of religious exaltation. *The Japanese Journal of Psyco-Analysis*, 1957, *4*, 1-9.

Prince, R. and Savage, C. Mystical states and the concept of regression. *Psychedelic Review*, 1966, *8*, 59-75.

Prince, R. Fundamental differences of psychoanalysis and faith healing. *International Journal of Psychiatry*, 1972, *10*, 125-128.

Rubins, J. L. Neurotic attitude toward religion. *American Journal of Psychoanalysis*, 1955, *15*, 71-81.

Saffady, W. Fears of sexual license during the English Reformation. *History of Childhood Quarterly*, 1973, *1*, 89-96.

Salzman, L. The psychology of religious and ideological conversion. *Psychiatry*, 1953, *16*, 177-187.

Salzman, L. Psychology of (regressive) religious conversion. *J. Pastoral Care*, 1954, *8*, 61-75.

Schroeder, T. (Rev. S. C.) Religious "Love in Action" (Introduction and interpolations). *Psychoanalytic Review*, 1925, *12*, 414-419.

Schroeder, T. Manufacturing "The Experience of God." *Psychoanalytic Review*, 1927, *14*, 71-84.

Schroeder, T. The psychoanalytic approach to religious experience. *Psychoanalytic Review*, 1929, *16*, 361-376.

Weininger, B. The interpersonal factor in the religious experience. *Psychoanalysis, Journal of the National Psychological Association for Psychoanalysis*, 1955, *3*, 27-44.

Wittels, F. A contribution to a symposium on religious art and literature. *Journal of the Hillside Hospital*, 1952, *1*, 3-6.

See also section 30.

## 33. RITUAL - GENERAL.

Bettelheim, B. *Symbolic Wounds: Puberty Rites and the Envious Male*. Glencoe, Illinois: Free Press, 1954.

Bonaparte, M. Notes on excision. In Roheim, G. (Ed.) *Psychoanalysis and the Social Sciences*. New York: International Universities Press, 1950, 2, 67-84.

Desmonde, W. H. The origin of money in the animal sacrifices. *Journal of the Hillside Hospital*, 1954, 3, 219-225.

Desmonde, W. H. *Magic, Myth and Money: The Origin of Money in Religious Ritual*. New York: Free Press of Glencoe, 1962, 208 p.

Devereux, G. and Mars, L. Haitian Voodoo and the ritualization of the nightmare. *Psychoanalytic Review*, 1951, 38, 334-342.

Dundes, A. Summoning deity through ritual fasting. *American Imago*, 1963, 20, 213-220.

Erikson, E. H. Ontogeny of ritualization. In R. M. Loewenstein et al. (Ed.) *Psychoanalysis - A General Psychology: Essays in Honor of Heinz Hartmann*. New York: International Universities Press, 1966.

Jones, I. H. Subincision among Australian western desert aborigines. *British Journal of Medical Psychology*, 1969, 42, 183-190.

La Barre, W. *They Shall Take Up Serpents*; Minneapolis: University of Minnesota Press, 1962.

Money-Kryle, R. E. *The Meaning of Sacrifice*. London: The Hogarth Press and the Institute of Psycho-Analysis, 1930, 273 p.

Posinsky, S. H. Ritual, neurotic and social. *American Imago*, 1962, 19, 375-390.

Reik, T. From spell to prayer. *Psychoanalysis*, 1955, 3, (1) 3-26.

Reik, T. *Ritual: Psycho-Analytic Studies.* New York: Norton, 1931, 367 p. With title: *The Psychological Problems of Religion.* New York: Farrar, Straus, 1946.

Reik, T. Puberty rites among savages. On some similarities in the mental life of savages and neurotics. In author's *Ritual, Psychoanalytic Studies,* 91-166.

Roheim, G. Dying gods and puberty ceremonies. *Journal of the Royal Anthropological Institute,* 1929, *59,* 181-197.

Roheim, G. *The Riddle of the Sphinx.* London: Hogarth Press, 1934.

Roheim, G. Transition rites. *Psychoanalytic Quarterly,* 1942, *11,* 336-374.

Sachs, H. The transformation of impulses into the obsessional ritual. *American Imago,* 1946, *3,* 67-74.

Schneiderman, L. A theory of repression in the light of archaic religion. *The Psychoanalytic Review,* 1966, *53,* 220-232.

Skinner, J. Ritual matricide: A study of the origins of sacrifice. *American Imago,* 1961, *18,* 71-102.

Stern, M. M. Ego psychology, myth and rite: Remarks about the relationship of the individual and the group. *The Psychoanalytic Study of Society,* 1964, *3,* 71-93.

Tarachow, S. Ambiguity and human imperfection. *Journal of the American Psychoanalytic Association,* 1965, *13,* 85-101.

Wayne, R. A little religious ceremonial. *American Imago,* 1954, *11,* 194-202.

Young, F. W. *Initiation Ceremonies: A Cross-Cultural Study of Status Dramatization.* Indianapolis: Bobbs-Merrill 1965, xiv + 199 p.

See also section 28.

## 33. CONTEMPORARY CULTS, SPIRITUALISM AND MAGIC.

Bonilla, E. S. Spiritualism, psychoanalysis, and psychodrama. *American Anthropologist*, 1969, *71*, 493-497.

Devereux, G. & Mars, L. Haitian Voodoo and the ritualization of the nightmare. *Psychoanalytic Review*, 1951, *38*, 334-342.

Kiev, A. Ritual goat sacrifice in Haiti. *American Imago*, 1962, *19*, 349-359.

Lawton, G. The psychology of spiritual mediums. *Psychoanalytic Review*, 1932, *19*, 418-445.

Lidz, R., Lidz, T. & Barton-Bradley, B. G. Cargo cultism: A psychosocial study of Melanesian millenarianism. *Journal of Nervous and Mental Disease*, 1973, *157*, 370-388.

# 34. EGO PSYCHOLOGY AND THE PSYCHOLOGY OF RELIGION.

Allison, J. Adaptive regression and intense religious experience. *Journal of Nervous and Mental Disease*, 1967, *145*, 452-463.

Allison, J. Religious conversion: Regression and progression in an adolescent experience. *Journal for the Scientific Study of Religion*, 1969, *8*, 23-38.

Almansi, R. J. Ego-psychological implications of a religious symbol: A cultural and experimental study. *The Psychoanalytic Study of Society*, 1964, *3*, 39-70.

Arlow, J. A. Ego-psychology and the study of mythology. *Journal of the American Psychoanalytic Association*, 1961, *9*, 371-393.

Arlow, J. A. The Madonna's conception through the ear. *The Psychoanalytic Study of Society*, 1964, *3*, 13-25.

Bergman, M. S. The impact of ego-psychology on the study of the myth. *American Imago,* 1966, *23*, 257-264.

Erikson, E. H. *Childhood and Society*. 2nd Ed. New York: Norton, 1963.

Panel, Mythology and ego psychology. *The Psychoanalytic Study of Society*, 1964, *3*, 4-87.

Stern, M. M. Ego psychology, myth, and rite: Remarks about the relationship of the individual and the group. *The Psychoanalytic Study of Society*, 1964, *3*, 71-93.

Tarachow, S. Mythology and ego psychology. *The Psychoanalytic Study of Society*, 1964, *3*, 9-12.

## 35. OBJECT RELATIONS THEORY AND THE PSYCHOLOGY OF RELIGION.

Balint, M. *Problems of Human Pleasure and Behavior.* New York: Liveright, 1957.

Dare, C. An aspect of the ego psychology of religion: A comment on Dr. Guntrip's paper. *British Journal of Medical Psychology*, 1969, *42*, 335-340.

Guntrip, H. J. S. *Personality Structure and Human Interaction.* New York: International Universities Press, 1961.

Guntrip, H. J. S. Religion in relation to personal integration. *British Journal of Medical Psychology*, 1969, *42*, 323-333.

Klein, M. *Contributions to Psychoanalysis, 1921-1945.* London: Hogarth Press, 1965.

Rizzuto, A. M. Object relations and the formation of the image of God. *British Journal of Medical Psychology*, 1974, *47*, 83-99.

Winnicott, D. W. *The Maturational Processes and the Facilitating Environment.* New York: International Universities Press, 1965.

## 36. TOTEMISM.

Desmonde, W. H. *Magic, Myth and Money: The Origin of Money in Religious Ritual.* New York: Free Press of Glencoe, 1962, 208 p.

Reik, T. *Dogma and Compulsion.* New York: International Universities Press, 1951.

Reik, T. The face of God. *Psychoanalysis,* 1955, *3,* (2), 3-26.

Reik, T. *Pagan Rites in Judaism.* New York: Farrar, Straus, 1964, 206 p.

Roheim, G. *Australian Totemism: A Psycho-Analytic Study in Anthropology.* London: Allen & Unwin, 1925, 487 p.

See also section 17.

## 37. ACADEMIC ("EMPIRICAL") STUDIES.

Beit-Hallahmi, B. and Argyle, M. God as a father projection: The theory and the evidence. *British Journal of Medical Psychology*, 1975, *48*, 71-75.

Bose, U. A psychological approach to the origin of religion and the development of the concepts of god and ghost in children. *Samiksa*, 1948, *2*, 25-64.

Deconchy, J. P. God and parental images: The masculine and feminine in religious free associations. In A. Godin (Ed.) *From Cry to Word.* Brussels: Lumen-Vitae, 1968.

Eisenman, R., Bernard, J. L. and Hannon, J. E. Benevolence, potency, and God: A semantic differential study of the Rorschach. *Perceptual and Motor Skills*, 1966, *22*, 75-78.

Godin, A. and Hallez, M. Parental images and divine paternity. In A. Godin (Ed.) *From Religious Experience to Religious Attitude.* Brussels: Lumen-Vitae, 1964.

Klausner, S. Z. Sacred and profane meanings of blood and alcohol. *Journal of Social Psychology*, 1964, *64*, 27-43.

Larsen, L. and Knapp, R. H. Sex differences in symbolic conceptions of the deity. *Journal of Projective Techniques and Personality Assessment*, 1964, *28*, 303-306.

Lesser, G. S. Religion and the defensive responses in children's fantasy. *Journal of Projective Techniques*, 1959, *23*, 64-68.

Nelson, M. O. The concept of God and feelings towards parents. *Journal of Individual Psychology.* 1971, *27*, 46-49.

Nelson, M. O. and Jones, E. M. An application of the Q-technique to the study of religious concepts. *Psychological Reports*, 1957, *3*, 293-297.

Siegman, A. W. An empirical investigation of the psychoanalytic theory of religiuos behavior. *Journal for the Scientific Study of Religion*, 1961, *1*, 74-78.

Spiro, M. E. and D'Andrade, R. G. A cross-cultural study of some supernatural beliefs. *American Anthropologist*, 1960, *60*, 456-466.

Strunk, O. Perceived relationships between parental and deity concepts. *Psychological Newsletter*, 1959, *10*, 222-226.

Tamayo, A. and Desjardines, L. Belief systems and conceptual images of parents and God. *Journal of Psychology*, 1976, *92*, 131-140.

Vergote, A. et al. Concept of God and parental images. *Journal for the Scientific Study of Religion*, 1969, *8*, 79-87.

Vergote, A. and Aubert, C. Parental images and representations of God. *Social Compass*, 1972, *19*, 431-444.

## 38. ATTEMPTS TO RECONCILE RELIGION AND PSYCHOANALYSIS.

Anonymous, Catholic Church and psychoanalysis, *American Journal of Psychotherapy*, 1952, 6, 435-439.

Apolito, A. Psychoanalysis and religion. *American Journal of Psychoanalysis*, 1970, 30, 115-126.

Bakan, D. Science, mysticism, and psychoanalysis. *Catholic Psychological Record*, 1966, 4, 1-9.

Barbour, C. E., *Sin and the new psychology*, New York: Abingdon, 1930, 269 p.

Bartemeir, L. H. Psychoanalysis and Religion, *Bulletin of the Menninger Clinic* 1965, 29, 237-244.

Bowers, M. L. Symbolism in worship. *Transactions* (Journal Dept. Psychiatry, Marquette School of Medicine) 1969, 1, 1-6.

Brav, A. Psychoanalysis in the light of religious experience. *Medical Review of Rev.*, 1935, 41, 612-621.

Brierley, M. Notes on psychoanalysis and integrative living *International Journal of Psychoanalysis*, 1947, 28, 218-224.

Carter, J. D. Maturity: Psychological and Biblical. *Journal of Psychology and Theology*, 1974, 2, 89-96.

Caruso, I. A. Sur la possibilite des influences positives de la psychanalyse sur la vie religieuse (on the possibility of some positive influences of psychoanalysis on religious life) *Supplement de la Vie Spirituelle*, 1958, 11, 5-20.

Caruso, I. A. Vie pulsionelle et religion (Life instinct and religion) *Revue de Psychologie et des Sciences de l'Education*, 1966-67, 2, 12-20.

Casey, R. P. Religion and psychoanalysis. *Psychiatry*, 1943, 6, 291-300.

Choisy, M. Symboles et mythes (Symbols and myths). *Psyche* - Paris, 1947, 2, 646 - 660.

Choisy, M. Les problemes que nous avons a resourdre en commun (The problems which we have to solve in common), *Psyche* - Paris, 1949, *4*, 313-334.

Choisy, M. Mythes d'hier et d'aujourd'hui (Myths of yesterday and today) *Psyche* - Paris, 1950, *5*, 290-303.

Choisy, M. Le discours de Souverain Pontife sur la psychotherapie (The Pope's speech on psychotherapy), *Psyche* - Paris, 1953, *6*, 145-155.

Choisy, M. *Le chretien devant la psychanalyse.* (The Christian before Psychoanalysis) Paris: Librarie P. Tequi, 1955, 216 p.

Choisey, M. Toute-puissance de la pensee et peche d'intention (Omnipotence of thought and the sin of intention) *Psyche* (Paris) 1955, *10,* 377-404.

Choisy, M. Psychoanalysis and Catholicism. In Birmingham W. & Cunseen J. *Cross Currents of Psychiatry and Catholic Morality* NY: Pantheon, 1964, 62-83.

Cole, W. G. *Sex in Christianity and Psychoanalysis.* NY: Oxford University Press, 1955; London: Allen & Unwin, 1957.

Combes, A. La psychanalyse freudienne et la religion chretienne. (Freudian psychoanalysis and the Christian religion) *La Table Ronde*, 1956.

Curran, P. J. Convergent and divergent views in the problem of religious confession and psychiatric treatment. *Bulletin Isaac Ray Medical Library*, 1954, *2*, 135-152.

Dempsey, P. J. R. *Freud, Psychoanalysis and Catholicism.* Chicago: H. Regnery, 1956, 209 p.

Doniger, S. (Ed.) *Religion and Human Behavior.* NY: Associated Press, 1954, xxii + 233 p.

Doniger, S. *Sex and Religion Today.* NY: Associated Press, 1953, 238 p.

Franzblau, A. N. Psychiatry and religion. In S. Noveck (Ed.) *Judaism and Psychiatry.* New York: Basic Books, 1956.

Fromm, E. *Psychoanalysis and Religion.* New Haven, Conn.: Yale University Press, 1950.

Fromm, E. Freud and Jung: it is a misleading oversimplification to say that Freud is a foe and Jung a friend of religion. *Pastoral Psychology*, 1950, *1*, 11-15.

Furlong, F. P. Peaceful coexistence of religion and psychiatry. *Bulletin of the Menninger Clinic*, 1955, *19*, 210-216.

Galdston, I. Psychiatry and religion. *Journal of Nervous and Mental Diseases*, 1950, *112*, 46-57.

Gassert, R. G. & Hall, B. H. *Psychiatry and Religious Faith*. New York: Viking Press, 1964, xx + 171 p.

Gemelli, A. *Psycho-Analysis Today*. (Tr. Chapin, J. S. & Ataanasio, S.) New York: P. J. Kenedy, 1955, 153 p.

Gilbert, A. L. The ecumenical movement and the treatment of nuns. *International Journal of Psycho-Analysis*, 1968, *49*, 481-483.

Ginsburg, S. W. Concerning religion and psychiatry. *Child Study*, 1953, *30*, 12-20.

Ginsburg, S. W. *Man's place in God's world, a psychiatrist's evaluation.* Cincinnati: Hebrew Union College, Jewish Institute of Religion, 1948, 30 p.

Glasner, S. Toward an operational definition of religion. In Wolff, W. *Psychiatry and Religion*, New York: MD Publications, 1955, 32-36.

Godin, A. Suicide ou sacrifice? (Suicide or sacrifice) *Psyche* - Paris, 1948, *31*, 1048-1063.

Gross, L. *God and Freud*. New York: David McKay, 1959.

Grotjahn, M. Psychoanalysis and faith: The thirty-year debate between Sigmund Freud and Oskar Pfister. In S Post (Ed.) *Moral Values and The Superego Concept in Psychoanalysis*. New York: International Universities Press, 1972.

Guirdham, A. *Christ and Freud: A Study of Religious Experience and Observance.* London: Allen & Unwin, 1959, 193 p.

Hacker, F. J. Scientific facts, religious values and the psychoanalytic experience. *Bulletin of the Menninger Clinic*, 1955, *19*, 229-239.

Hiltner, S. Religion and psychoanalysis. *Psychoanalytic Review*, 1950, *37*, 128-139.

Hiltner, S. Some contribution of psychoanalysis to religious understanding. *Complex*. Spring, 1952, *8*, 28-40.

Hiltner, S. Psychiatry and religion. *Pastoral Psychology*, 1954, *5*, 8-9.

Hiltner, S. Psychiatry and thoughts on God. *Bulletin of the Menninger Clinic*, 1955, *19*, 217-226.

Hiltner, S. Erich Fromm and pastoral psychology. *Pastoral Psychology*, 1955, *6*, 11-12.

Hiltner, S. Freud, Psychoanalysis and religion. *Pastoral Psychology*, 1956, *7*, 9-21.

Hinkle, B. M. The spiritual significance of psychoanalysis. *British Journal of Psychology*, 1921-1922, *2*, 209-230.

Homans, P. *Theology after Freud*. Indianapolis: Bobbs-Merrill, 1970.

Hsu, Francis L. K. *Religion, Science and Human Crises*. London: Routledge & Kegan Paul, 1952, 142 p.

Jager-Werth, U. Oskar Pfister and the beginnings of religious socialism. *Journal of Religion and Health*, 1974, *13*, 57-61.

Jores, A. The original sin of mankind: an attempt at a psychological interpretation. In Belgum, D. *Religion and Medicine*. Ames: Iowa State University Press, 1967, 135-143.

Kaplan, A. Maturity in religion. *Bulletin of the Philadelphia Association for Psychoanalysis* 1963, *13*, 101-119.

Knight, J. A. Calvinism and psychoanalysis: a comparative study. *Pastoral Psychology*, 1963, *14*, 10-17.

Knight, J. A. *A Psychiatrist Looks at Religion and Health*. New York: Ashville: Abington Press, 1964, 207 p.

Knight, J. A. Religious - psychological conflicts of the adolescent. In Usdin, G. L. *Adolescence*, Phila: Lippincott, 1967, 31 - 50.

Knight, J. A. Adolescent development and religious values. *Voices*, 1969, *4*, 68-72.

Leavy, S. A. The psychic function of religion in mental illness and health. *Group for the Advancement of Psychiatry Rep.*, 1968, *67*, 647-730.

Lee, R. S. *Freud and Christianity*. New York: A. A. Wyn, 1949, 204 p.

Lemercier, G. Freud in the cloister: interview. *Atlas*, 1967, *13*, 33-37.

Lepp, I. *The Depths of the Soul: A Christian Approach to Psychoanalysis*. Staten Island, N. Y. : Alba House, 1966, 280 p.  Garden City, N. Y.: Image Books, 1967, 274 p.

Linn, L. & Schwartz, L. W. *Psychiatry and Religious Experience*. New York: Random House, 1958, 307 p.

Linn, L. On the difference between psychiatry and religion. In Noveck, S. *Judaism and Psychiatry*, New York: Basic Books, 1956.

Linn, L. The boundary line between psychiatry and religion. In Noveck S. (Ed.) *Judaism and Psychiatry*, 177-181.

Linn, L. The need to believe. In Noveck S. *Judaism and Psychiatry*, 129-134.

Loomis, E. A. Jr. *The Self in Pilgrimage*. New York: Harper, 1969, xvii + 104 p.

Lubin, A. J. A psychoanalytic view of religion. In E. M. Pattison (Ed.) *Clinical Psychiatry and Religion*. Boston: Little Brown & Co., 1969.

Maguire, J. D. Theological uses of psychoanalysis: patterns, problems, and proposals. *Religion in Life, 1962, 31*, 169-184.

Mailloux, N. Obstacles to the realisation of the ascetic ideal. In : *Christain Asceticism and Modern Man*. New York: Philo Library, 1955, 237-252.

Mailloux, N. Psychology and spiritual direction. In Braceland, F. J. *Faith, Reason and Modern Psychiatry*. New York: Kennedy, 1955, 247-263.

Mailoux, N. Religious and moral issues in psychotherapy and counseling. *Ann. NY Academy of Science*, 1955, *63*, 427-428.

Malev, M. The value of ritual . In Noveck, S. *Judaism and Psychiatry*, 135-142. New York: Random HOuse, 1956.

Malony, H. N. & North, G. The future of an illusion and the illusion of a future. *Journal of the History of the Behavioral Sciences*, in press.

McNeill, Harry V. Freudians and Catholics. *The Commonwealth*, 1947, *46*, 350-353.

Menninger, K. A. Psychiatry looks at religion. *A Psychiatrist's world: Selected Papers*, 793-802.

Meyerhoff, H. By love redeemed. A fantasy on "God and Freud", *Commentary*, 1959, *2*, 202-206.

Meyerson, O. G. & Stoller, L. A psychoanalytic interpretation of the crucifixion. *Psychoanalysis and the Psychoanalytic Review*, 1962, *49*, 117-118.

Mollegen, A. T. A Christian view of psychoanalysis, *Christianity and Psychoanalysis*. Wash: Organizing Committee, Christianity and Modern Life, 1952, 1-18.

Moore, T. V. Religion, Psychiatry and mental hygiene. *Psychiatry*, 1944, 7, 321-326.

Mowrer, O. The unconscious re-examined in a religious context. In Strunk, O. Jr. (Ed.) *Readings in the Psychology of Religion.* Nashville, Tenn.: Abingdon Press, 1959.

Mowrer, O. H. Psychopathology and the problems of guilt, confession, and expiation. In Dennis, W. et al. *Current Trends in Psychological Theory*, Pittsburgh: University of Pittsburgh Press, 1961, 208-229.

Mowrer, O. H. Sigmund Freud: psychopathologist or "theologian" *Psychiatric Digest*, 1965, *26*, 39 - 46.

Murphy, G. Religion and the social sciences. *Religion* (Kansas) 1968, *5*, 1-4.

Noveck, S. *Judaism and Psychiatry. Two Approaches to the Personal Problems and Needs of Modern Man.* New York: Basic Books, 1956, xiii + 197 p.

O'Doherty, E. F. Toward a dynamic psychology. Freud and St. Thomas. *Studies*, 1960, *49*, 341-354.

Ostow, M. Religion and morality: A psychoanalytic view. In S. Post (Ed.) *Moral Values and the Superego Concept in Psychoanalysis.* New York: Int. Univ. Press, 1972.

Ostow, M. Religion and psychoanalysis: the area of common concern. *Pastoral Psychology*, 1959, *10*, 33-38.

Paddock, F. A philosophical investigation of the relation between psychoanalysis and theology. *Journal of Pastoral Care*, 1959, *13*, 38-41.

Pasquarelli, B. Psychoanalysis and religion - a postulated autonomy in function. *Bulletin of the Philadelphia Association for Psychoanalysis*, 1960, *10*, 10-17.

Pattison, E. M. (Ed.) *Clinical Psychiatry and Religion*. International Psychiatry Clinics. Vol. 5. (4) Boston: Little, Brown, 1969, xii, 327 p.

Ple', A. St. Thomas and the psychology of Freud. Dominican Studies, 1952. In Birmingham, W. & Cunneed, J. E. *Cross Currents of Psychiatry and Catholic Morality*. New York: Pantheon Books, 1964, 84-109.

Price, R. Fundamental differences of psychoanalysis and faith healing. *International Journal of Psychiatry*, 1972, *10*, 125-128.

Proust, M. Freud et Saint Paul (Freud and St. Paul) *Psyche* - Paris, 1947, *2*, 464-467.

Ross, J. H. A current psychoanalytic concept of God. *International Record of Medicine*, 1955, *168*, 760-767.

Runestam, A. *Psychoanalysis and Christianity*, (Tr. Winfield O.) Rock Island, Ill.: Augustana Press, 1958, 194 p.

Sanders, B. G. *Christianity after Freud; an Interpretation of the Christian Experience in the Light of Psycho-Analytic Theory*. London: Bles, 1949, New York: Macmillan, 1949, 157 p.

Smith, V. E. The study of man: an essay in reconstruction. In Braceland, J. J. *Faith, Reason and the Modern Psychiatry*. New York: Kennedy, 1955, 145-179.

Sapirstein, M. R. The meaning of personal religious experience. In Noveck, S. (Ed.) *Judaism and Psychiatry*, 119-127.

Schnaper, N. & Schnaper, H. W. A few kind words for the devil. *Journal of Religion and Health*, 1969, *8*, 107-122.

Shaw, D. The Christian roots of psychoanalysis. In *Christianity and Modern Man*. Washington: 1952, 51-56.

Silverberg, W. V. Psychoanalysis, religion and world crisis. *Holy Cross Magazine*, 1942, *53*, 195-198.

Steinbach, A. A. Can psychiatry and religion meet? In Noveck, S. (Ed.) *Judaism and Psychiatry*, 169-176.

Stern, K. Psychiatry and religion. *Hospital Progress*, St. Louis, 1955, *36*, 62-63.

Stern, K. *The Third Revolution. A Study of Psychiatry and Religion*. New York: Harcourt Brace, 1954, 306 p.

Stern, K. Some spiritual aspects of psychotherapy. In Braceland, F. J. *Faith, Reason and Modern Psychiatry*. New York: Kennedy, 1955, 125-140.

Stevenson, I. P. Assumptions of religion and psychiatry. *Bulletin of the Menninger Clinic*, 1955, *19*, 199-209.

vander Veldt, J. H. & Odenwald R. P. *Psychiatry and Catholicism*. New York: Toronto, London: McGraw Hill, 1952, 433 p.

Walker, K. Psychology and religion. *Hibbert Journal*, 1961, *60*, 10-15.

Walters, O. S. Metaphysics, religion and psychotherapy. *Journal of Counseling Psychology*, 1958, *5*, 243-252.

Walters, O. S. Theology and changing concepts of the unconscious. *Religion In Life*, 1968, *37*, 112-128.

Want, R. L. Psychoanalysis and religion. *Australasian Journal of Philosophy*, 1939, *17*, 241-250.

Westendrop, F. The value of Freud's illusion. *Journal of Psychology and Theology*, 1975, *3*, 82-89.

Wile, I. S. Psychoanalysis and religion. *Mental Hygiene*, 1932, *16*, 529-563.

Witcutt, W. P. *Catholic Thought and Modern Psychology*. London: Burns, Oates and Washbourne, 1948, 1944, 57 p.

Wolff, W. Introduction to the symposium on psychiatry and religion. *Psychiatry and Religion*. 1-2.

Wolff, W. *Changing Concepts of the Bible. A Psychological Analysis of Its Word, Symbols and Beliefs.* New York: Hermitage House, 1951, 473 p.

Wolff, W. *Psychiatry and Religion.* New York: MD Publications, 1956, 62 p.

Wolff, W. Symposium on psychiatry and religion. Introduction. *International Record of Medicine*, 1955, *168*, 767-768.

Wolman, B. B. (Ed.) *Psychoanalysis and Catholicism.* New York: Gardner Press, 1976.

Woodward, L. E. Fostering mental health through the church program in Maves, P. B. *The Church and Mental Health.* New York, London. Scribner's, 1953, 129-157.

Zilboorg, G. A response. *Psychoanalytic Quarterly*, 1944, *13*, 93-100.

Zilboorg, G. Psychiatry and religion. *Atlantic Monthly*, 1949, *183*, 47-50.

Zilboorg, G. *Psychoanalysis and Religion.* New York: Barnes & Noble, 1950.

Zilboorg, G. *Freud and Religion: A Restatement of an Old Controversy.* Westminster, Md: Newman Press, London: Geoffrey Chapman, 1958, 65 p.

Zilboorg, G. Psychoanalysis and religion. *Pastoral Psychology*, 1959, *10*, 41-48.

Zilboorg, G. *Psychoanalysis and Religion.* New York: Farrar, Straus & Cudahy, 1962, xi + 243 p.

See also section 39.

## 39. PSYCHOANALYTIC INFLUENCES ON PASTORAL COUNSELING.

Allport, G. W. Behavioural science, religion, and mental health. In Belgum, D. *Religion and Medicine.* Ames, Iowa: Iowa State University Press, 1967, 83-95.

Blanton, S. Freud and theology. *Pastoral Counselor*, 1963, *1*, 3-8.

Booth, G. Unconscious motivation in the choice of the ministry as vocation. *Pastoral Psychology*, 1958, *9*, 18-24.

Bowers, M. K. & Bigham, T. J. The cross as a command to suffer. *International Record of Medicine*, 1958, *171*, 753-760.

Bowers, M. K. Protestantism in its therapeutic implications. *Annual Psychotherapy Monogram no. 2, New York:* American Academy of Psychotherapy, 1959.

Bowers, K. Psychotherapy of religious personnel: some observations and recommendations. *Journal of Pastoral Care*, 1963, *17*, 11-16.

Bowers, K. Psychotherapy of religious conflict. *International Psychiatry Clinics,* 1969, *5*, 233-242.

Bowers, K., Berkowitz, B., and Brecher, S. Therapeutic implications of analytic group psychotherapy of religious personnel. *International Journal of Group Psychotherapy*, 1958, *8*, 243-256.

Colm, H. N. Psychotherapy and the ground of being. *Psychoanalysis and the Psychoanalytic Review*, 1960, *47*, 115-117.

Cossa, P. Le medicin catholique devant la psychanalyse; methodes et doctrines. (Catholic medicine before psychoanalysis: methods and doctrines). *Bulletin of Social Medicine S. Luc.*, 1937, *43*, 3-33.

De Foust, I. Gold, frankincense and myrrh. *Child Family Digest*, 1954, *10*, 3-9.

Ford, J. C. May Catholics be psychoanalyzed? *Pastoral Psychology*, 1954, *5*, 25-34.

Franzblau, A. N. Contribution of Psychiatry to religious education. *Journal of Religious Education*, 1956, *51*, 335-338.

Galdston, I. (Ed.) *Ministry and Medicine in Human Relations.* New York: International Universities Press, 1955, 173 p.

Godin, A. Conscience humaine et techniques psychologique. (Human consciousness and psychological techniques) *Rev. ge'n Belg*, 1956, *92*, 610-622.

Gross, L. *God and Freud*. New York: McKay, 1957.

Guntrip, H. J. S. *Psychology for Ministers and Social Workers*. London: Independant Press, 1949, 356 p. Chicago: Allenson, 1953.

Guntrip, H. J. S. *Mental Pain and the Cure of Souls.* London: Independant Press, 1956, 206 p. with title *Psychotherapy and Religion.* New York: Harper, 1957, 206 p.

Guntrip, H. J. S. Psychotherapy and Religion: The constructive use of inner conflict. *Pastoral Psychology*, 1957, *8*, 31-40.

Helweg, H. *Soul Sorrow: The Psychiatrist Speaks to the Minister*. New York: Pagenat Press, 1955, 151 p.

Hesnerd, A. L. M. Le drame de l'aveu (The drama of confession). *Psyche* - Paris, 1949, *4*, 94-104.

Hiltner, S. The contribution of religion to mental health. *Mental Hygiene*, 1940, *24*, 366-377.

Hiltner, S. *Pastoral Counseling*. New York: Abingdon-Cokesbury Press, 1949.

Hiltner, S. Pastoral theology and psychology. *Protestant thought in the Twentieth Century*, New York: McMillan, 1951, 181-199.

Hiltner, S. Christian faith and psychotherapy. *Religion in Life*, 1952, *2*, 492-501.

Hiltner, S. Pastoral psychology and pastoral counseling in Doniger, S. *Religion and Human Behavior*. New York: Association Press, 1954, 179-195.

Hiltner, S. Freud for the Pastor. *Pastoral Psychology*. 1955, *5*, 41-57.

Hiltner, S. Pastoral care and counseling. *Journal of Religious Thought*, 1956, *13*, 111-122.

Hiltner, S. An appraisal of pastoral psychology today. *Pastoral Psychology*, 1957, *6*, 9-10.

Hiltner, S. A program in religion and psychiatry. *Bulletin of the Menninger Clinic*, 1959, *23*, 217-225. *Pastoral Psychology*, 1960, *11*, 12-18.

Hiltner, S. psychiatry and Christian hope. *Pastoral Psychology*, 1969, *11*, 7-9.

Hiltner, S. & Ziegler, J. H. Clinical pastoral education and the schools. *Journal of Pastoral Care*, 1961, *15*, 129-143.

Hiltner, S. The dialogue on man's nature. In Doniger, S. *The Nature of Man*, New York: Harper, 1962, 237-261.

Hiltner, S. An appraisal of religion and psychiatry since 1954. *Journal of Religious Health*, 1965, *4*, 217-226.

Hiltner, S. Clinical psychology and religion in Riess, B. & Abt, L. E. (Eds.) *Progress in Clinical Psychology*. New York: Grune & Stratton, 1966, 7, 129-150.

Homans, P. *Theology after Freud.* Indianapolis: Bobbs-Merrill, 1970.

Kew, C. W. & Kew, C. J. Principles and values of group psychotherapy under church auspices. *Pastoral Psychology*, 1955, *6*, 37-48.

Kew, C. E. & Kew, C. J. Writing as an aid in pastoral counseling and psychotherapy. *Pastoral Psychology*, 1963, *14*, 37-43.

Knight, J. A. Partners in healing. *Pulpit Digest*, 1964, Oct., 11-18.

Knight, J. A. Church phobia. *Pastoral Psychology*, 1967, *18*, 33-38.

Knight, J. The use and misuse of religion by the emotionally disturbed. *Pastoral Psychology*, 1962, *13*, 10-18.

Lopez, I. J. Angoisse ve cue et vocation religieuse (Experience of anxiety and religious vocation). *Psyche* - Paris, 1954, *9*, 443-446.

Loomis, E. A. Jr. Religion and Psychiatry in Deutsch A. & Fishman, H. (Eds.) *The Encyclopedia of Mental Health.* New York: Franklin Watts, 1963, 1965, 1748-1759.

Loomis, E. A. Jr. Psychiatry and the Christian ministry. *Union Theological Semi Quarterly Review*, 1957, *12*, 31-39.

May, R. Religious psychotherapy and achievement of selfhood. *Pastoral Psychology*, 1951, *2*, 15-20.

May, R. Forward to Guntrip, H. *Psychotherapy and Religion*, 7-10.

Menninger, K. Psychoanalysis and the ministry. *Pastoral Psychology*, 1958, *9*, 59.

Menninger, K. & Pruyser, P. W. Religious and spiritual values. In Doniger, S. *Becoming the Complete Adult.* New York: Associated Press, 1962, 95-118.

Miller, Samuel H. Exploring the boundary between religion and psychiatry. *Journal of Pastoral Care*, 1952, *6*, 1-11.

Mollegen, A. F. Utilization of religious attitudes in clinical psychiatry. *Bulletin Isaac Ray Medical Library*, 1954, *2*, 116-135.

Niebuhr, U. M. Sex in Christianity and psychoanalysis. *Religion in Life*, 1956, *25*, 613-618.

Nodet, C. H. Considerations psychoanalytiques a propos des attraits nerotiques pour la vie religieuse. (Psychoanalytic considerations regarding neurotic attractions to the religious life) *Supplement de la Vie Spirituelle*, 1954, *28*, 53-63.

Oates, W.*The Christian Pastor*, Philadelphia: Westminster Press, 1951.

Outler, A. C. *Psychotherapy and the Christian Message.* New York. Harper, 1954.

Parrot, P. & Romain, R. P. Maturite affective et vocation sacerdotale. (Affective maturity and the vocation of priesthood). *Supplement de la Vie Spirituelle*, 1958, *46*, 307-322.

Pattison, E. M. On the failure to forgive or to be forgiven. *American Journal of Psychotherapy*, 1965, *19*, 106-115.

Putnam, J. J. The service to nervous invalides of the physician and the minister. *Havard Theological Review*, 1909, April 1.

Roberts, D. E. *Psychotherapy and a Christian View of Man*. New York: Scribner's, 1953.

Sutherland, R. L. Therapeutic goals and ideals of health. *Journal of Religion and Health*, 1964, *3*, 119.

Sutherland, R. L. The pastor and the mental health team. *Journal of Religion and Health*, 1964, *4*, 22.

Tillich, P. The meaning of health. *Perseption Biological Medicine*, 1961, *5*, 92-100. In Belgum, D. *Religion and Medicine*, Ames, Iowa: Iowa State University Press, 1967, 3-12.

Trueblood, D. E. The challenge of Freud. *Pastoral Psychology*, 1958, *9*, 37-44.

Watson, A. S. The fear of faith. *Pastoral Psychology*, 1963, *139*, 18-26.

Weigert, E. V. The contribution of pastoral counseling and psychotherapy to mental health. *British Journal of Medical Psychology*, 1960, *33*, 269-273.

Young, D. R. Pastoral counseling in the church? *Journal of Religious Health*, 1964, *3*, 353-358.

Zilboorg, G. Scientific Psychotherapy and religious issues. *Theological Studies*, 1953, *14*, 288-297.

Zilboorg, G. Some denials and assertations of religious faith in Braceland, F. J. *Faith, Reason and Modern Psychiatry*. New York: Kennedy, 1955, 99 121.

Zilboorg, G. Is religion a cure for neurosis? *Bulletin Guild Catholic Psychiatrists*, 1958, *6* (1).

See also section 38.

## KEY TO SUBJECT LISTINGS.

1. BIBLIOGRAPHIES.
2. PERIODICAL REVIEWS.
3. FREUD ON RELIGION: THE ORIGINAL WRITINGS.
4. FREUD ON RELIGION: ADDITIONAL SOURCES.
5. GENERAL DISCUSSIONS AND CRITICAL REVIEWS.
6. AFRICAN RELIGIONS.
7. AMERINDIAN AND ESKIMO RELIGIONS.
8. ANCIENT NEAR EAST RELIGIONS.
9. BUDDHISM AND HINDUISM.
10. CHRISTIANITY - GENERAL.
11. CHRISTIANITY - ARTIFACTS.
12. CHRISTIANITY - DOGMA.
13. CHRISTIANITY - HOLIDAYS AND FESTIVALS.
14. CHRISTIANITY - MYTHOLOGY.
15. CHRISTIANITY - RITUAL.
16. CHRISTIANITY - SECTS.
17. "PRIMITIVE" RELIGION.
18. GREEK RELIGION AND MYTHOLOGY.
19. ISLAM.
20. JUDAISM - GENERAL.
21. JUDAISM - ARTIFACTS.
22. JUDAISM - DOGMA.
23. JUDAISM - HOLIDAYS AND FESTIVALS.
24. JUDAISM - MYTHOLOGY.
25. JUDAISM - RITUAL.
26. FREUD, JUDAISM AND PSYCHOANALYSIS.
27. MYTHOLOGY - GENERAL AND COMPARATIVE.

28. ORIGINS OF RELIGION.
29. PREHISTORICAL RELIGIONS.
30. RELIGION, PERSONALITY, AND PSYCHOPATHOLOGY.
31. RELIGIOUS THINKING AND RELIGIOUS EXPERIENCE.
32. RITUAL - GENERAL.
33. CONTEMPORARY CULTS, SPIRITUALISM AND MAGIC.
34. EGO PSYCHOLOGY AND THE PSYCHOLOGY OF RELIGION.
35. OBJECT RELATIONS THEORY AND THE PSYCHOLOGY OF RELIGION.
36. TOTEMISM.
37. ACADEMIC ("EMPIRICAL") STUDIES.
38. ATTEMPTS TO RECONCILE PSYCHOANALYSIS AND RELIGION.
39. PSYCHOANALYTIC INFLUENCES ON PASTORAL COUNSELING.

# ALPHABETICAL LISTING AND INDEX.

The sections where the entry appears are indicated by numbers in brackets following the entry.

Abraham, K. Amenhotem IV: A psychoanalytic contribution to the understanding of his personality and the monotheistic cult of Athon. *Psychoanalytic Quarterly*, 1935, *4*, 537-569. [8]

Abraham, K. Dreams and myths (1909). In K. Abraham *Clinical Papers and Essays on Psychoanalysis*. New York: Basic Books, 1955. [27]

Abou, Z. La psychanalyse des mythes. *Egyptian Journal of Psychology*, 1946, *2*, 233-251. [27]

Ackerman, N. W. and Jahoda, M. *Anti-Semitism and Emotional Disorder: A Psychoanalytic Interpretation*. New York: Harper, 1950. [20]

Alexander, F. Buddhistic training as an artificial catatonia. *The Psychoanalytic Review*, 1931, *18* 129-145. [9]

Allison, J. Adaptive regression and intense religious experience. *Journal of Nervous and Mental Disease*, 1967, *145*, 452-463. [31, 34]

Allison, J. Religious conversion: Regression and progression in an adolescent experience. *Journal for the Scientific Study of Religion*, 1969, *8*, 32-28. [31, 34]

Allport, G. W. Behavioral science, religion, and mental health. In Belgum, D. *Religion and Medicine*. Ames, Iowa: Iowa State University Press, 1967, 83-95. [39]

Almansi, R. J. A psychoanalytic interpretation of the Menorah. *Journal of the Hillside Hospital*, 1953, *2*, 80-95. [21]

Almansi, R. J. Applied psychoanalysis: Religion, mythology and folklore. In Frosch, J. (Ed.) *The Annual Survey of Psychoanalysis*. 1953, *4*, 340-355. [2]

Almansi, R. J. Applied psychoanalysis: Religion, mythology and folklore. In J. Frosch (Ed.) *The Annual Survey of Psychoanalysis*, 1954, *5*, 438-457. [2]

Almansi, R. J. A further contribution to the psychoanalytic interpretation of the Menorah. *Journal of the Hillside Hospital*, 1954, *3*, 3-18. [21]

Almansi, R. J. Applied psychoanalysis, I: Mythology and folklore. In Frosch, J. (Ed.) *The Annual Survey of Psychoanalysis*. New York: International Universities Press, 1956, *7*, 376-383. [2]

Almansi, R. J. Applied psychoanalysis, I: Religion, mythology and folklore. In Frosch, J. *The Annual Survey of Psychoanalysis*. New York: International Universities Press, 1957, *8*, 296-310. [2]

Almansi, R. J. Applied psychoanalysis, I: Religion, mythology and folklore. In Frosch, J. (Ed.) *The Annual Survey of Psychoanalysis*, 1958, *9*, 439-449. [2]

Almansi, R. J. Ego-psychological implications of a religious symbol: A cultural and experimental study. *The Psychoanalytic Study of Society*, 1964, *3*, 39-70. [20, 34]

Amsel, A. *Judaism and Psychology*. New York: Philipp Feldheim, 1969, xv + 213 p. [26]

Anderson, F. A. Psychopathological glimpses of some biblical characters. *The Psychoanalytic Review*, 1927, *14*, 56-70. [24]

Anonymous. Catholic Church and psychoanalysis. *American Journal of Psychotherapy*, 1952, *6*, 435-439. [38]

Apolito, A. Psychoanalysis and religion. *American Journal of Psychoanalysis*, 1970, *30*, 115-126. [5, 38]

Argyle, M. and Beit-Hallahmi, B. *The Social Psychology of Religion*. London: Routledge & Kegan Paul, 1975. [28]

Arlow, J. A. A psychoanalytic study of a religious initiation rite. *The Psychoanalytic Study of the Child*, 1951, *6*, 353-374. [25]

Arlow, J. A. The consecration of the prophet. *Psychoanalytic Quarterly*, 1951, *20*, 374-397. [24]

Arlow, J. A. Applied psychoanalysis: Religion. In Frosch, J. (Ed.) *The Annual Survey of Psychoanalysis*, 1951, 2, 538-553. [2]

Arlow, J. A. Ego psychology and the study of mythology. *Journal of the American Psychoanalytic Association*, 1961, 9, 371-393. [27, 34]

Arlow, J. A. The Madonna's conception through the ear. *The Psychoanalytic Study of Society*, 1964, 3, 13-25. [14, 27, 30, 34]

Aron, W. Freudiana, Judaica. *Jewish Forum.* New York: 1956, June: 98-99, August: 104-105, September: 138-139. [26]

Bakan, D. Freud's Jewishness and his psychoanalysis. *Judaism*, 1954, 3 (1), 20-26. [26]

Bakan, D. *Sigmund Freud and the Jewish Mystical Tradition.* Princeton, New Jersey: Van Nostrand, 1958, xix + 326 p. [26]

Bakan, D. Some thoughts on reading Augustine's "Confessions." *Journal for the Scientific Study of Religion*, 1965, 5, 149-152. [30]

Bakan, D. *The Duality of Human Existence.* Chicago: Rand McNally, 1966. [5, 10, 20]

Bakan, D. Science, mysticism, and psychoanalysis. *Catholic Psychological Record*, 1966, 4, 1-9. [38]

Bakan, D. *Disease, Pain, and Sacrifice: Toward a Psychology of Suffering.* Chicago: University of Chicago Press, 1968, 134 p. [5]

Balint, M. *Problems of Human Pleasure and Behavior.* New York: Liveright, 1957. [30, 35]

Balter, L. The mother as a source of power: A psychoanalytic study of three Greek myths. *Psychoanalytic Quarterly*, 1969, 38, 217-274. [18]

Banks, R. Religion as projection. *Religious Studies*, 1973, 9, 401-426. [5]

Barag, G. The mother in the religious concepts of Judaism. *American Imago*, 1946, 4, 32-53. [22, 24]

Barag, G. The question of Jewish monotheism. *American Imago*, 1947, *4*, 8-25. [22, 24]

Barande, R. La "pulsion de mort" comme nontransgression: Survie et transfiguration du tabou de l'inceste (The "death-drive" as nontransgression: Survival and transfiguration of the incest taboo). *Revue Francaise de Psychanalyse*, 1968, *32*, 465-502. [28]

Barbour, C. E. *Sin and the new psychology*. New York: Abingdon, 1930, 269 p. [38]

Barnes, F. F. The myth of the seal ancestors. *The Psychoanalytic Review*, 1953, *40*, 156-157. [7, 28]

Barnouw, V. A psychological interpretation of a Chippewa origin legend. *Journal of American Folklore*, 1955, *68*, 73-85, 211-223, 341-355. [7, 27]

Bartemeier, L. H. Psychoanalysis and Religion. *Bulletin of the Menninger Clinic*, 1965, *29*, 237-244. [38]

Baruk, H. La Signification de la psychanalyse et le judaisme. (The significance of psychoanalysis and Judaism). *Review Historical Medical Hebrew*, 1966, *19*, 15-29, 53-65, 131-132. [26]

Baudouin, C. Signification des fetes (The meaning of festivities). *Psyche* - Paris, 1947, *2*, 1291-1308. [13]

Baudouin, C. Le Saint precepteur du Diablo (The Saint tutor of the Devil). *Psyche* - Paris, 1949, *4*, 351-357. [14]

Baudouin, C. La sublimation des images chex Huysmans lors de sa conversion (Sublimation of images in Huysmans at the time of his religious conversion). *Psyche* - Paris, 1959, *5*, 378-385. [30]

Baudouin, C. *Psychanalyse de Symbole Religieuse*. Paris: Fayard, 1957. [5, 27]

Beck, S. J. Abraham's ordeal: Creation of a new reality. *Psychoanalytic Review*, 1963, *50*, 334-349. [24]

Beck, S. J. Cosmic optimism in some Genesis myths. *American Journal of Orthopsychiatry*, 1971, *41*, 380-389. [24]

Becker, E. A note on Freud's primal horde theory. *Psychoanalytic Quarterly*, 1961, *30*, 413-419. [28]

Beidelman, T. O. The ox and Nuer sacrifice: Some Freudian hypotheses about Nuer symbolism. *Man*, 1966, *1*, 453-467. [6]

Beirnaert, L. Le role affectif de la Vierge - Mere dans le catholicisme (The emotional role of the virgin-mother in Catholicism). *Psyche* - Paris, 1947, *2*, 1309-1318. [14]

Beirnaert, L. Freud, la religion et la civilisation (Freud, religion and civilization). In *Problemes de Psychanalyse*, Paris: Fayard, 1957, 173-183. [5]

Beirnaert, R. P. L. Psychanalyse et symbolisme religieux (Psychoanalysis and religious symbolism). *Cahiers Laennec*, 1948, *8*, 42-50. [5]

Beit-Hallahmi, B. Sacrifice, fire, and the victory of the sun: A search for the origins of Hanukkah. *Psychoanalytic Review*, 1977, *63*, 497-509. [13, 23]

Beit-Hallahmi, B. and Argyle, M. God as a father projection: The theory and the evidence. *British Journal of Medical Psychology*, 1975, *48*, 71-75. [5, 28, 37]

Beit-Hallahmi, B. and Paluszny, M. Twinship in mythology and science: Ambivalence, differentiation, and the magical bond. *Comprehensive Psychiatry*, 1974, *15*, 345-353. [27]

Bellah, R. N. Father and son in Christianity and Confucianism. *The Psychoanalytic Review*, 1965, *52*, 92-114. [9. 14. 27]

Benassy, M. Psychanalyses didactiques et experiences religieuses (Training psychoanalyses and religious experiences). *Revue Francaise de Psychanalyse*, 1965, *29*, 31-41. [31]

Beres, D. Psychoanalytic notes on the history of morality. *Journal of the American Psychoanalytic Association*, 1965, *13*, 337. [28]

Bergman, M. S. The impact of ego psychology on the study of the myth. *American Imago*, 1966, *23*, 257-264. [27, 34]

Bergman, P. A religious conversion in the course of psycotherapy. *American Journal of Psychotherapy*, 1953, 7, 41-58. [31]

Berkeley-Hill, O. The anal-erotic factor in the religion, philosophy, and the character of the Hindus. *International Journal of Psychoanalysis*, 1921, 2, 306-338. [9]

Berkower, L. The enduring effect of the Jewish tradition upon Freud. *American Journal of Psychiatry*, 125, 1067-1075. [26]

Bettelheim, B. *Symbolic Woulds: Puberty Rites and the Envious Male*. Glencoe, Illinois: Free Press, 1954. [32]

Bidner, D. So-called primitive medicine and religion. In Gladston, I. (Ed.) *Man's Image in Medicine and Anthropology*. New York: International Universities Press, 1963. [5, 17]

Bimer, L. The first foreign land. *Psychoanalytic Review*, 1971, 58, 303-309. [13]

Binswanger, L. *Sigmund Freud: Reminiscences of a Friendship*. New York: Grune & Stratton, 1957. [4]

Bjerre, P. C. The way to grace. *The Psychoanalytic Review*, 1927, 14, 255-267. [31]

Blanton, S. Freud and theology. *Pastoral Counselor*, 1963, 1, 3-8. [39]

Block, S. L. St. Augustine: On grief and other psychological matters. *American Journal of Psychiatry*, 1966, 122, 943-946. [30]

Blum, F. H. Psychoanalysis and religion (A historical view of Freud). In Wolff, W. *Psychiatry and Religion*. New York: MD Publications, 1955, 8-13. [5]

Boas, F. The methods of ethnology. *American Anthropologist*. New Series, 1920, 22, 319-321. [5]

Bonaparte, M. Universal myths. In Lorland, S. (Ed.) *The Yearbook of Psychoanalysis*. New York: International Universities Press, 1946. [27]

Bonaparte, M. Saint Christopher patron saint of the motor-car drivers. *American Imago*, 1947, 4, 49-77. [14]

Bonaparte, M. Notes on excision. In Roheim, G. (Ed.) *Psychoanalysis and the Social Sciences.* New York: International Universities Press, 1950, *2*, 67-84. [32]

Bonaparte, M. Eros, Saul de Tarse et Freud. *Revue Francaise de Psychanalyse*, 1957, *21*, 23-33. [10]

Bonaparte, M. Psycho-analysis in relation to social, religious and natural forces. *International Journal of Psycho-Analysis*, 1958, *39*, 513-515. [5]

Bonilla, E. S. Spiritualism, psychoanalysis and psychodrama. *American Anthropologist*, 1969, *71*, 493-497. [33]

Booth, G. Unconscious motivation in the choice of the ministry as vocation. *Pastoral Psychology*, 1958, *9*, 18-24. [39]

Bose, U. A psychological approach to the origin of religion and the development of the concepts of god and ghost in children. *Samiksa*, 1948, *2*, 25-64. [37]

Bowers, M. K. Protestantism in its therapeutic implications. *Ann. Psychotherapy Monograph. no. 2.* New York: American Academy of Psychotherapy, 1959. [39]

Bowers, M. K. Psychotherapy of religious personnel: Some observations and recommendations. *Journal of Pastoral Care*, 1963, *17*, 11-16. [39]

Bowers, M. K. Psychotherapy of religious conflict. *International Psychiatry Clinics*, 1969, *5*, 233-242. [39]

Bowers, M. K. Symbolism in worship. *Transactions* (Journal of Department of Psychiatry, Marquette School of Medicine), 1969, *1*, 1-6. [38]

Bowers, M. K. and Bigham, T. J. The cross as a command to suffer. *International Record of Medicine*, 1958, *171*, 753-760. [39]

Bowers, M. K. , Berkowitz, B., and Brecher, S. Therapeutic implications of analytic group psychotherapy of religious personnel. *International Journal of Group Psychotherapy*, 1958, *8*, 243-256. [39]

Boyer, L. B. Christmas 'Neurosis.' *Journal of the American*

*Psychoanalytic Association*, 1955, *3*, 467-488. [13]

Boyer, L. B. Stone as a symbol in Apache mythology. *American Imago*, 1965, *22*, 14-39. [7]

Boyer, L. B. and Boyer, R. M. A combined anthropological and psychoanalytic contribution to folklore. *Psychopathologie Africaine*, 1967, *3*, 333-372. [27]

Bradley, N. Primal scene experience in human evolution and its phantasy derivatives in art, proto-science and philosophy. In Muensterberger, W. and Axelrad, S. (Eds.) *The Psychoanalytic Study of Society*. New York: International Universities Press, 1967, *4*, 34-79. [28]

Brandt, R. J. Freud and Nietzsche: A comparison. *Review of the University of Ottawa*, 1955, *25*, 225-234. [5]

Brav, A. Psychoanalysis in the light of religious experience. *Medical Review of Reviews*, 1935, *41*, 612-621. [38]

Brend, W. A. *Sacrifice to Attis. A study of sex and civilization*. London. Toronto: Heinemann, 1936, 350 p. [8]

Brenner, A. B. Some psychoanalytic speculations on Anti-Semitism. *Psychoanalytic Review*, 1948, *35*, 20-32. [20]

Brenner, A. B. The great mother goddess: Puberty initiation rites and the covenant of Abraham. *The Psychoanalytic Review*, 1950, *37*, 320-340. [20, 24]

Brenner, A. B. The covenant with Abraham. *The Psychoanalytic Review*, 1952, *39*, 34-52. [20, 24]

Brenner, A. B. Onan, the levirate marriage and the genealogy of the Messiah. *Journal of the American Psychoanalytic Association*, 1962, *10*, 701-721. [24]

Brenner, C. *An Elementary Textbook of Psychoanalysis*. Garden City, New York: Doubleday, 1974. [5]

Brierly, M. Notes onpsychoanalysis and integrative living. *International Journal of Psychoanalysis*, 1947, *28*, 218-224. [38]

Brill, A. A. Thoughts on life and death, on Vidonian All Soul's eve. *Psychiatric Quarterly*, 1947, *21*, 199-211. [28]

Brink, L. Frazer's *Folklore in the Old Testament.* A critical review. *The Psychoanalytic Review*, 1922, *9*, 218-254. [20]

Brodbeck, A. J. Religion and art as socializing agencies: A note on the revision of Marxist and Freudian theories. *Psychological Reports*, 1957, *3*, 161-165. [5]

Brody, M. Phylogenesis of sexual morality: Psychiatric exegesis on Onan and Samson. *New York State Journal of Medicine*, 1968, *68*, 2510-2512. [20, 24]

Brown, N. O. *Life Against Death*. Middletown, Connecticut: Wesleyan University Press, 1958. [5]

Brown, N. O. *Love's Body*. New York: Random House, 1966. [5]

Bunker, H. A. The feast of Tantalus. *Psychoanalytic Quarterly*, 1952, *21*, 355-372. [18]

Bunker, H. A. Tantalus: A preoedipal figure of myth. *Psychoanalytic Quarterly*, 1953, *22*, 159-173. [18]

Bunker, H. A. The Bouphonia, or ox-murder: A footnote to *Totem and Taboo. Psychoanalysis and the Social Sciences*, 1947, *1*, 165-169. [28]

Bunker, H. A. Psychoanalysis and the study of religion. In G. Roheim (Ed.) *Psychoanalysis and the Social Sciences*. Vol. III. New York. International Universities Press, 1951. [5]

Burke, K. *The Rhetoric of Religion: Studies in Logology*. Boston: Beacon Press, 1961, vi + 327 p. [5]

Bychowski, G. The ego and the introjects: Origin of religious experience. *Psychoanalysis and the Social Sciences*, 1958, *5*, 246-279. [28]

Cafferata, R. F., S. J. L'influence du surmoi dans la formation religieuse (The influence of the super-ego in the molding of religious feeling). *Psyche* - Paris, 1949, *4*, 413-422. [30]

Campbell, J. Bios and Mythos. Prolegomena to a science of mythology. In Wilbur, G. and Muensterberger, W. (Eds.) *Psychoanalysis and Culture*. New York: International Universities Press, 1961. [27]

Campbell, J. *The Hero with a Thousand Faces*. New York: Pantheon Books, 1949, xxiii + 416 p. [27]

Campbell, J. *The Masks of God: Primitive Mythology*. New York: Viking, 1959, 504 p. [27]

Campbell, J. (Ed.) *Man and Transformation*. (Tr: Manheim, R.). New York: Pantheon Books, 1964, xviii + 413 p. [27]

Campbell, J. (Ed.) *Myths, Dreams and Religion*. New York: E. P. Dutton & Co., 1970, 355 p. [27]

Campbell, J. *The Flight of the Garden: Explorations in the Mythological Dimension*. 2nd Ed. Chicago: Henry Regenry Co., 1972, 248 p. [27]

Capps, D., Rambo, L. and Ransohoff, P. *Psychology of Religion: A Guide to Information Sources*. Detroit: Gale, 1976. [1]

Caprio, F. S. Ethnological attitudes toward death; a psychoanalytic evaluation. *Journal of Clinical Psychopathology*, 1946, 7, 737-752. [5]

Carter, J. D. Maturity; Psychological and Biblical. *Journal of Psychology and Theology*, 1974, 2, 89-96. [38]

Caruso, I. A. Sur la possibilite des influences positives de la psychanalyse sur la vie religieuse (On the possibility of some positive influences of psychoanalysis on religious life). *Supplement de la Vie Spirituelle*, 1958, *11*, 5-20. [38]

Caruso, I. A. Vie pulsionelle et religion (Instinct life and religion). *Revue de Psychologie et des Sciences de l'Education*, 1966-67, 2, 12-20. [38]

de Carvalho-Netto, P. *Folklore and Psychoanalysis*. Coral Gables, Florida: University of Miami Press, 1972. [27]

Casey, R. P. The psychoanalytic study of religion. *Journal of Abnormal and Social Psychology*, 1938, *33*, 437-452. [5]

Casey, R. P. Oedipus motivation in religious thought and fantasy. *Psychiatry*, 1942, *5*, 219-228. [28]

Casey, R. P. Religion and psychoanalysis. *Psychiatry*, 1943, *6*, 291-300. [38]

Casey, R. P. Psychoanalytic study of religion. In Strunk, O. *Readings in the Psychology of Religion*. New York: Abingdon Press, 1959, 62-74. [5]

Chandler, T. Ikhnaton and Moses. *American Imago*, 1962,

*19*, 127-139. [8, 20]

Charny, E. J. The confessions of St. Augustine. *Psychiatric Communications*, 1958, *1*, 101-111. [30]

Chassel, J. O. Freudianism and religion. *Methodist Review*, 1922, July, 507-524. [5]

Chasseguet-Smirgel, J. Oedipe et religion (Oedipus and religion). *Revue Francaise de Psychanalyse*, 1967, *31*, 875-882. [28]

Chaudhuri, A. K. R. A psychoanalytic study of the Hindu mother goddess (Kali) concept. *American Imago*, 1956, *13*, 123-145. [9]

Choisy, M. Symboles et mythes (Symbols and myths). *Psyche* - Paris, 1947, *2*, 646-660. [38]

Choisy, M. Les problemes que nous avons a resourdre en commun (The problems which we have to solve in common). *Psyche* - Paris, 1949, *4*, 313-334. [38]

Choisy, M. Mythes d'hier et d'aujourd'hui (Myths of yesterday and today. *Psyche* - Paris, 1950, *5*, 290-303. [38]

Choisy, M. Le discours de Souverain Pontife sur la psychotherapie (The Pope's speech on psychotherapy). *Psyche* - Paris, *1953, 6, 145-155. [38]*

Choisy, M. *Le chretien devant la psychanalyse* (The Christian before psychoanalysis). Paris: Librarie P. Tequi, 1955, 216 p. [38]

Choisy, M. Toute-puissance de la pensee et peche d'intention (Omnipotence of thought and the sin of intention). *Psyche* - Paris, 1955, *10*, 377-404. [38]

Choisy, M. Psychoanalysis and Catholicism. In Birmingham W. and Cureen, J. *Cross Currents of Psychiatry and Catholic Morality*. New York: Pantheon, 1964, 62-83. [38]

Cohen, M. B. Psychoanalysis and religion. *Psychiatry*, 1952, *15*, 219-220. [5]

Cohen, S. B. The ontogenesis of prophetic behavior: A study in creative conscience formation. *Psychoanalysis and the Psychoanalytic Review*, 1962, *49*, 100-122. [30, 31]

Cohn, N. The cult of the free spirit: A medieval heresy reconstructed. *Psychoanalysis and the Psychoanalytic Review*, 1961, *48*, 51-68. [10]

Cole, W. G. *Sex in Christianity and Psychoanalysis*, New York: Oxford University Press, 1966. [5, 12, 38]

Colm, H. N. Religious symbolism in child analysis. *Psychoanalysis, Journal of the National Psychological Association for Psychoanalysis*, 1953, *2*, 39-56. [30]

Colm, H. N. Psychotherapy and the ground of being. *Psychoanalysis and the Psychoanalytic Review*, 1960, *47*, 115-117. [39]

Cologeras, R. C. Levi-Strauss and Freud: Their 'structural' approaches to myth. *American Imago*, 1973, *30*, 57-79. [27]

Combes, A. La psychanalyse freudienne et la religion chretienne (Freudian psychoanalysis and the Christian Religion). *La Table Ronde*, 1956, December (108), 88. [38]

Condon, W. S. Psychoanalysis and civilization. *Psychiatric Commentary*, 1960, 5-20. [5]

Coriat, I. H. A note on the sexual symbolism of the Cretan snake goddess. *Psychoanalytic Review*, 1917, *4*, 367-368. [8]

Cossa, P. Le medicin catholique devant la psychanalyse; methodes et doctrines (Catholic medicine before psychoanalysis; Methods and doctrines). *Bulletin of Social Medicine S. Luc.*, 1937, *43*, 3-33. [39]

Coster, G. *Psychoanalysis for Normal People*. London: Oxford University Press, 1926, 1927, 232 p.; 1942, viii + 227 p. London, New York: Oxford University Press, 1947, viii + 227 p. [5]

Cox, H. L. The place of mythology in the study of culture. *American Imago*, 1948, *5*, 83-94. [27]

Cronbach, A. Psychoanalysis and Religion. *Journal of Religion*. 1922, *2*, 588-599. [2]

Cronbach, A. Religion and psychoanalysis. *Psychological*

*Bulletin*, 1926, *23*, 701-713. [2]

Cronbach, A. The psychology of religion. A bibliographical survey. *Psychological Bulletin*, 1928, *25*, 701-719. [2]

Cronbach, A. The psychoanalytic study of Judaism. *Hebrew Union College Annual*, 1931-32, *8-9*, 605-740. [20]

Cronbach, A. The psychology of religion. *Psychological Bulletin*, 1933, *30*, 327-361. [2]

Cronbach, A. New Studies in the psychology of Judaism. *Hebrew Union College Annual*, 1946, *19*, 205-273. [20]

Cronin, H. J. Psychoanalytic sources of religious conflicts. *Medicl Record*, 1934, *139*, 32-34. [30]

Curran, F. J. Convergent and divergent views in the problem of religious confession and psychiatric treatment. *Bulletin of Isaac Ray Medical Library*, 1954, *2*, 135-152. [38]

Dalmau, C. J. Anthropocentric aspects of religion. *The Psychoanalytic Review*, 1967, *54*, 679-687. [28]

Daly, C. D. The psycho-biological origins of circumcision. *International Journal of Psychoanalysis*, 1950, *31*, 217-236. [25]

Dare, C. An aspect of the ego psychology of religion: A comment on Dr. Guntrip's paper. *British Journal of Medical Psychology*, 1969, *42*, 335-340. [5, 35]

Darlington, H. S. The confession of sins. *Psychoanalytic Review*, 1937, *24*, 150-164. [31]

Davy, M. M. Des limites de la psychanalyse a la forme de la mystique (Limitations of psychoanalysis to the form of the mystique). *Psyche*, 1949, *4*, 105-116. [38]

Day, F. The future of psychoanalysis and religion. *The Psychoanalytic Quarterly*. 1944, *13*, 84-92. [5]

Deconchy, J. P. God and parental images: The masculine and feminine in religious free associations. In A. Godin (Ed.) *From Cry to Word*. Brussels: Lumen-Vitae, 1968. [37]

De Foust, I. Gold, frankincense and myrrh. *Child Family Digest*, 1954, *10*, 3-9. [39]

Deikman, A. J. De-automatization and the mystic experience. *Psychiatry*, 1966, *24*, 324-338. [31]

Dempsey, P. J. R. *Freud, Psychoanalysis, and Catholicism.* Chicago: H. Regnery, 1956, 209 p. [38]

Desmonde, W. H. The murder of Moses. *American Imago*, 1950, 7, 351-367. [20]

Desmonde, W. H. The bull fight as a religious ritual. *American Imago*, 1952, 9, 173-195. [8, 18, 29]

Desmonde, W. H. The Eleusian mysteries. *Journal of the Hillside Hospital*, 1952, 1, 204-218. [18]

Desmonde, W. H. The eternal fire as a symbol of the state. *Journal of the Hillside Hospital*, 1953, 2, 143-147. [28, 29]

Desmonde, W. H. The origin of money in the animal sacrifices. *Journal of the Hillside Hospital*, 1954, 3, 219-225. [32]

Desmonde, W. H. *Magic, Myth and Money: The Origin of Money in Religious Ritual.* New York: Free Press of Glencoe, 1962, 208 p. [32, 36]

Deutsch, H. *A Psychoanalytic Study of the Myth of Dionysus and Apollo.* New York: International Universities Press, 1969, 101 p. [18]

Devereux, G. Belief, superstition, and symptom. *Samiksa*, 1954, 8, 210-215. [31]

Devereux, G. Dream learning and individual differences in Mohave shamanism. *American Anthropologist*, 1957, 59, 1036-1045. [7]

Devereux, G. and Mars, L. Haitian Voodoo and the ritualization of the nightmare. *Psychoanalytic Review*, 1951, 38, 334-342. [32, 33]

Dillistone, F. W. *Christianity and Symbolism.* London: Collins, 1955, 320 p. [5]

Doniger, S. *Sex and Religion Today.* New York: Association Press, 1953, 238 p. [38]

Doniger, S. (Ed.) *Religion and Human Behavior.* New York: Association Press, 1954, xxii + 233 p. [38]

Dorsey, J. M. Some considerations of the psychoanalytical principle and religious living. *Samiksa*, 1954, 8, 47-57; 93-124. [5]

Dorson, R. M. Theories of myth and the folklorist. *Daedalus*, 1959, *88*, 280-290. [27]

Douglas, M. *Purity and Danger: An Analysis of Concepts of Pollution and Taboo*. London: Routledge & Kegan Paul, 1966, viii + 188 p. [17, 22]

Duff, I. F. G. A psychoanalytical study of a phantasy of St. Therese de l'enfant Jesus. *British Journal of Medical Psychology*, 1925, *5*, 345-357. [30]

Dundes, A. Earth diver: Creation of the mythopoeic male. *American Anthropologist*, 1962, *64*, 1032-1051. [7]

Dundes, A. The father, the son and the holy Grail. *Literature and Psychology*, 1962, *12*, 101-112. [14]

Dundes, A. Summoning deity through ritual fasting. *American Imago*, 1963, *20*, 213-220. [32]

Dundes, A. The hero pattern and the life of Jesus. Colloquy 25. The Center for Hermeneutical Studies. The Graduate Theological Union and the University of California, Berkeley, 1977. [14]

Edelheit, H. Mythopoesis and the primal scene. *Psychoanalytic Study of Society*, 1972, *5*, 212-233. [27]

Edelheit, H. Crucifixion fantasies and their relation to the primal scene. *International Journal of Psycho-Anaysis*, 1974, *55*, 193-199. [14]

Eder, M. D. The Jewish phylacteries and other Jewish ritual observances. *International Journal of Psycho-Analysis*, 1933, *14*, 341-375. [21, 25]

Eisenbud, J. Negative reactions to Christmas. *Psychoanalytic Quarterly*, 1941, *10*, 639-645. [13, 31]

Eiseman, R., Bernard, J. L. and Hannon, J. E. Benevolence, potency, and God: A semantic differential study of the Rorschach. *Perceptual and Motor Skills*, 1966, *22*, 75-78. [37]

Eisler, E. R. The religious factor in mental disorder. *Journal of Abnormal Psychology*, 1924-25, *19*, 85-95. [30]

Eissler, K. R. Appendix 2. Further notes on the religious controversy. In *Medical Orthodoxy and the Future of Psy-*

*choanalysis.* New York: International Universities Press, 1965. [5]

Ekstein, R. A clinical note on the therapeutic use of a quasi-religious experience. *Journal of the American Psychoanalytic Association*, 1956, *4*, 304-313. [31]

Eliade, M. *Myths, Dreams and Mysteries*, New York: Harper, 1960. [27]

Eliade, M. *Images and Symbols: Studies in Religious Symbolism.* (Tr: Mariet, P.) New York: Sheed and Ward, 1961, 189 p. [5]

Eliade, M. *Myth and Reality.* New York: Harper, 1963. [27]

Erikson, E. H. *Young Man Luther, A Study in Psychoanalysis and History.* New York: W. W. Norton, 1958, 288 p. [30]

Erikson, E. H. *Childhood and Society*, 2nd Ed. New York: Norton, 1963. [5, 34]

Erikson, E. H. Ontogeny of ritualization. In R. M. Loewenstein et al. (Ed.) *Psychoanalysis - A General Psychology: Essays in Honor of Heinz Hartmann.* New York: International Universities Press, 1966. [32]

Evans, W. N. Notes on the conversion of John Bunyan: A study in English Puritanism. *International Journal of Psychoanalysis*, 1943, *24*, 176-185. [30]

Fairbairn, W. R. D. Notes on the religious fantasies of a female patient. In *An Object-Relations Theory of the Personality*. New York: Basic Books, 1954, pp. 183-196. [30]

Farrell, B. A. Psychological theory and the belief in God. *International Journal of Psycho-Analysis*, 1955, *36*, 187-204. [5]

Feiner, A. H. and Levenson, E. A. The compassionate sacrifice: An explanation of a metaphor. *The Psychoanalytic Review*, 1968-69, *55*, 552-573. [5, 31]

Feldman, A. A. Freud's *Moses and Monotheism* and the three stages of Israelitic religion. *Psychoanalytic Review*, 1944, *31*, 361-418. [20]

Feldman, A. A. The Davidic dynasty and the Davidic Messiah. *American Imago*, 1960, *17*, 163-178. [24]

Feldman, A. B. Freudian theology. Part I. *Psychoanalysis*, 1952, *1* (1), 31-52. [5]

Feldman, A. B. Freudian theology. Part II. *Psychoanalysis*, 1953, *1* (2), 37-53. [5]

Feldman, A. B. Animal magnetism and the mother of Christian science. *The Psychoanalytic Review*, 1963, *50*, 313-320. [16]

Feldman, A. B. The word in the beginning. *The Psychoanalytic Review, 1964,* 51, *79-98. [28]*

Feldman, S. Notes on the primal horde. *Psychoanalysis and the Social Sciences*, 1947, *1*, 171-194. [28]

Feldman, S. S. The blessing of the Kohenites. *American Imago*, 1941, *2.* 296-322. [25]

Feldman, S. S. The sin of Reuben, first-born son of Jacob. In W. Munsterberger and S. Axelrad (Eds.) *Psychoanalysis and the Social Sciences.* Vol. IV. New York: International Universities Press, 1955. [24]

Feldman, S. S. Notes on some religious rites and ceremonies. *Journal of the Hillside Hospital*, 1959, *8*, 36-41. [25]

Fenichel, O. Psychoanalysis of antisemitism. *American Imago*, 1940, *1*, 24-39. [20]

Ferenczi, S. Obsessional neurosis and piety. In *Further Contributions to Psychoanalysis.* London: Hogart Press, 1926. [28]

Fingert, Hyman H. Psychoanalytic study of the minor prophet, Jonah. *The Psychoanalytic Review*, 1954, *41*, 55-65. [24]

Fisher, D. J. Sigmund Freud and Romain Rolland: The terrestrial animal and his great oceanic friend. *American Imago*, 1976, *33*, 1-59. [4, 5, 31]

Fitzherbert, J. The source of man's 'intimations of immorality.' *British Journal of Psychiatry*, 1964, *110*, 859-862. [38]

Flugel, J. C. *Man, Morals and Society*. New York: International Universities Press, 1945. [5, 28]

Fodor, A. The origin of the Mosaic prohibition against cooking the suckling in its mother's milk. *International Journal of Psychoanalysis*, 1946, *27*, 140-144. [22]

Fodor, A. Was Moses an Egyptian? *Psychoanalysis and the Social Sciences*, 1951, *3*, 189. [24]

Fodor, A. Asherah of Ugarit. *American Imago*, 1952, *9*, 118-146. [8]

Fodor, A. The fall of man in the book of Genesis. *American Imago*, 1954, *11*, 201=231. [24]

Fodor, N. A personal analytic approach to the problem of the Holy Name. *Psychoanalytic Review*, 1944, *31*, 165-180. [22]

Fodor, N. The hound of heaven. *Psychoanalysis*, 1955, *3*, 45-49. [14]

Fodor, N. Jung's sermons to the dead. *The Psychoanalytic Review*, 1964, *51*, 74-78. [30]

Ford, J. C. May Catholics be psychoanalyzed? *Pastoral Psychology*, 1954, *5*, 25-34. [39]

Fortes, M. *Oedipus and Job in West African Religion*. New York: Cambridge University Press, 1959. [6]

Fox, R. Totem and Taboo reconsidered. In E. R. Leach (Ed.) *The Structural Study of Myth and Totemism*. London: Tavistock, 1967. [28]

Foxe, A. N. Post-homicidal contrition and religious conversion. *Psychiatric Quarterly*, 1943, *17*, 565-578. [30]

Fraenkel, E. La circoncision chez les Juifs peut-elle s'expliquer comme une castration attenuee, infliquee a ses fils par le chef de la horde. *Psyche*, 1952, *7*, 377-385. [25]

Fraiberg, L. and Fraiberg, S. Hallowe'en: Ritual and myth in a children's holiday. *American Imago*, 1950, *7*, 289-327. [13]

Franzblau, A. N. Contribution of psychiatry to religious education. *Journal of Religious Education*, 1956, *51*, 335-338. [39]

Franzblau, A. N. Conversion, psychologically speaking. In Eichhorn, D. M. *Conversion to Judaism: A History and Analysis*. New York: Ktav Publishers, 1965, 189-207. [31]

Franzblau, A. N. Judaism and psychoanalysis. *Dimension*, 1967, *1*, 15-20, 30-31. [20]

Franzblau, A. N. Psychiatry and religion. In Noveck, S. (Ed.) *Judaism and Psychiatry*, 183-192. [5, 38]

Freehof, S. W. Three psychiatric stories from Rabbinic lore. *Psychoanalytic Review*, 1942, *29*, 185-187. [24]

Freeman, D. Totem and Taboo: A reappraisal. *The Psychoanalytic Study of Society*, 1965, *4*, 9-33. [28]

Freeman, D. Thunder, blood and nicknaming God's creatures. *The Psychoanalytic Quarterly*, 1968, *37*, 353-399. [5, 17]

Freeman, T. Some notes on a forgotten religion. *The Psychoanalytic Review*, 1954, *41*, 9-28. [8]

Freemantle, A. The Oedipal legend in Christian hagiology. *Psychoanalytic Quarterly*, 1950, *19*, 408-409. [10]

Freud, E. L. Reply to Naftalin, M. "Footnote to the Genesis of Moses" in the Psychoanalytic Quarterly, 1958, 27, 403-405. *The Psychoanalytic Quarterly*, 1959, *28*, 146. [4]

Freud, S. From *The Standard Edition of the Complete Psychological Works of Sigmund Freud*. (J. Strachey, Ed.). London: The Hogarth Press, 1953-1974. Entries listed according to date of original writing and volume.

| | |
|---|---|
| 1893a | On the psychical mechanism of hysterical phenomena. *2*, 1-18, 1955. [3] |
| 1893b | Charcot. *3*, 7-24, 1962. [3] |
| 1901 | *The Psychopathology Of Everyday Life*. *6* 1-290, 1960. [3] |
| 1905 | Fragment on an analysis of a case of hysteria. *7*, 1-122, 1953. [3] |
| 1907 | Obsessive actions and religious practices. *9*, 116-129, 1959. [3] |
| 1909a | Analysis of a phobia in a five year old boy. *10*. 1-150, 1955. [3] |

| | |
|---|---|
| 1909b | Notes upon a case of obsessional neurosis. *10*, 151-318, 1955. [3] |
| 1910a | *Leonardo da Vinci and a Memory of His Childhood. 11*, 59-138, 1957. [3] |
| 1910b | The future prospects of psychoanalytic therapy *11*, 139-152, 1957. [3] |
| 1911a | Psychoanalytic notes on an autobiographical account of a case of paranoia (Dementia Paranoides). *12*, 1-84, 1958. [3] |
| 1911b | Formulations on the two principles of mental functioning. *12*, 213-226, 1958. [3] |
| 1911c | 'Great is Diana of the Ephesians'. *12*, 342-344, 1958. [3] |
| 1913 | *Totem and Taboo. 13*, 1-164, 1955. [3] |
| 1914a | The Moses of Michaelangelo. *13*, 211-236. [3] |
| 1914b | On the history of the psychoanalytic movement. *14*, 1-66, 1957. [3] |
| 1915 | Thoughts for the time on war and death. *14*, 273-300, 1957. [3] |
| 1918 | From the historty of an infantile neurosis. *17*, 1-122. [3] |
| 1919 | Psychoanalysis and religious origins. Preface to T. Reik, *Ritual: Psychoanalytic Studies*. 17, 257-266, 1955. [3] |
| 1921 | *Group Psychology and the Analysis of the Ego. 18*, 65-144, 1955. [3] |
| 1923a | The ego and the id. *19*, 1-59, 1961. [3] |
| 1923b | A seventeenth-century demonological neurosis., *19*, 67-108, 1961. [3] |
| 1924 | A short account of psychoanalysis, *19*, 191-212, 1961. [3] |
| 1925 | Letter to the director of the Judische Presszentrale, Zurich *19*, 291, 1961. [26] |
| 1925 | On the Occasion of the opening of the Hebrew University. *19*, 292. 1961. [26] |

1925    An autobiographical study. *20*, 1-74, 1959. [3, 26]

1926    Address to members of the B'nai B'rith. *20*, 271-276, 1959. [26]

1927    *The Future of An Illusion. 21*, 1-56, 1961. [3]

1928a   Dostoevsky and parricide. *21*, 177-196, 1961. [3]

1928b   A religious experience. *21*, 167-174, 1961. [3]

1930    *Civilization and Its Discontents. 21*, 57-146, 1961. [3]

1932    The acquisition and control of fire. *22*, 183-194, 1964. [3]

1933    *New Introductory Lectures On Psychoanalysis.* 22, 1-82, 1964. [3]

1934    Preface to the Hebrew translation of Totem and Taboo. *13*, xv, 1955. [26]

1939    *Moses and Monotheism. 23*, 1-138, 1964. [3]

Freud, S. *The letters of Sigmund Freud* (Ed: Freud, E. L.). (Tr: Stern, T. and Stern, J.) New York: Basic Books, 1960, viii + 470 p. [26]

Freund, K. *Myths of Creation.* New York: Washington Square Press, 1965, vi + 304 p. [27]

Freund, K. The meaning of myth to modern man. *Journal of the Otto Rank Association*, 1967, *2*, 52-53. [27]

Fromm, E. Faith as a character trait. *Psychiatry*, 1942, *5*, 307-319. [28]

Fromm, E. Freud and Jung: It is a misleading oversimplification to say that Freud is a foe and Jung a friend of religion. *Pastoral Psychology*, 1950, *1*, 11-15. [38]

Fromm, E. *Psychoanalysis and Religion.* New Haven: Yale, 1950. [5, 38]

Fromm, E. *The Forgotten Language: An Introduction to the Understanding of Dreams, Fairy Tales and Myths.* New York: Rinehart, 1951, vii + 263 p. [27]

Fromm, E. Psychoanalysis and Zen Buddhism. In D. T. Suzuki (Ed.) *Zen Buddhism and Psychoanalysis.* New York: Grove Press, 1963. [9]

Fromm, E. *The Dogma of Christ and Other Essays on Religion, Psychology and Culture.* London: Routledge, 1963, 151 p. New York / Chicago / San Francisco: Holt Rinehart & Winston, 1963, 1964, x + 212 p. New York: Doubleday, 1966, ix + 213 p. [5]

Fromm, E. The dogma of Christ. *The Dogma of Christ and Other Essays on Religion, Psychology and Culture,* 3-91. New York: Holt, 1963. [12]

Fromm, E. *You Shall Be As Gods: A Radical Interpretation of the Old Testament and Its Tradition.* New York: Holt, Rinehart and Winston, 1966, 240 p.

Furlong, F. P. Peaceful coexistence of religion and psychiatry. *Bulletin of the Menninger Clinic,*, 1955, *19*, 210-216. [38]

Galdston, I. (Ed.) *Ministry and Medicine in Human Relations.* New York: International Universities Press, 1955, 173 p. [39]

Galdston, I. Psychiatry and religion. *Journal of Nervous and Mental Diseases,* 1950, *112*, 46-57. [38]

Garma, A. The origin of clothes. *The Psychoanalytic Quarterly,* 1949, *18*, 173-190. [21]

Gassert, R. G. and Hall, B. H. *Psychiatry and Religious Faith* (Foreward: Menninger, K.) New York: Viking Press, 1964, xx + 171 p. With title: *Mental Health and Religious Faith.* London: Darton, Longman & Todd, 1966, xviii + 171 p. [38]

Gedo, J. E. Mythopoesis and psychoanalysis. *American Imago,* 1970, *27*, 329-337. [27]

Gemelli, A. *Psycho-Analysis Today* (Tr. Chapin, J. S. and Attanasio, S.) New York: P. J. Kennedy, 1955, 153 p. [38]

Gilbert, A. A rabbinic theory of instincts. *Psychoanalysis, Journal of the National Psychological Association for Psycho-*

*analysis*, 1955, *3*, 36-43. [20]

Gilbert, A. L. The ecumenical movement and the treatment of nuns. *International Journal of Psycho-Analysis*, 1968, *49*, 481-483. [38]

Ginsburg, S. W. Man's place in God's world, a psychiatrist's evaluation. Cincinnati: Hebrew Union College, Jewish Institute of Religion, 1948, 30 p. In Kurth, G. and Herma, H. (Eds.) *Elements of Psychoanalysis*, Cleveland, Ohio: World Publishing Company, 1950, 279-296. [38]

Ginsburg, S. W. Concerning religion and psychiatry. *Child Study*, 1953, *30*, 12-20. [38]

Glasner, S. Toward an operational definition of religion. In Wolff, W. *Psychiatry and Religion*. New York: MD Publications, 1955, 32-36. [38]

Glenn, J. Circumcision and anti-Semitism. *Psychoanalytic Quarterly*, 1960, *29*, 395-399. [20]

Glover, E. *Freud or Jung*. New York: Norton, 1950. [5]

Glueck, B. The God man or Jehovah complex. *New York Medical Journal*, 1915, *102*, 496-499. [30]

Godin, A. Suicide ou sacrifice? (Suicide or sacrifice) *Psyche - Paris*, 1948, *3*, 1048-1063. [38]

Godin, A. Conscience humaine et techniques psychologiques (Human consciousness and psychological techniques). *Revue gen Belg.*, 1956, *92*, 610-622. [39]

Godin, A. and Hallez, M. Parental images and divine paternity. In A. Godin (Ed.) *From Religious Experience to Religious Attitude*. Brussels: Lumen Vitae, 1964. [37]

Goitein, L. The importance of the Book of Job for analytic thought. *American Imago*, 1954, *11*, 407-415. [20]

Goitein, L. Green Pastures: Psalm xxiii. *American Imago*, 1956, *13*, 409-414. [20]

Gonen, J. Y. Then men said, "Let us make God in our image after our likeness." *Literature and Psychology*, 1971, *21*, 69-79. [24]

Goodich, M. Childhood and adolescence among thirteenth century saints. *History of Childhood Quarterly*, 1973, *1*, 285-309. *[30]*

Gordon, K. H., Jr. Religious prejudice in an eight year old boy. *The Psychoanalytic Quarterly*, 1965, *34*, 102-107. [30]

Gordon, R. *Stereotype of Imagery and Belief as an Ego Defense*. New York: Cambridge University Press, 1962, vii + 96 p. [31]

Graves, R. and Patai, R. Some Hebrew myths and legends. *Encounter*, 1963, *20*, 3-18, *20* (3), 12-18. [24]

Greenacre, P. A study on the nature of inspiration. I. Some special considerations regarding the phallic phase. *Journal of the American Psychoanalytic Association*, 1964, *12*, 6-31. [30]

Greenberger, B. The anti-Semite and the oedipal conflict. *International Journal of Psychoanalysis*, 1964, *45*, 380-385. [20]

Gressot, M. Le mythe dogmatique et le systeme moral des manicheens. *Revue Francaise de Psychanalyse*, 1953, *17*, 398-427. [8]

Grinberg, L. Psychoanalytic considerations on the Jewish Passover: Totemic sacrifice and meal. *Aerican Imago*, 1962, *19*, 391-424. [25]

Grinstein, A. Stages in the development of control over fire. *International Journal of Psycho-Analysis*, 1952, *33*, 416-420. [27]

Grinstein, A. *The Index of Psychoanalytic Writings*. New York: International Universities Press, 1956-1973. [1]

Grinstein, A. *Sigmund Freud's Writings: A Comprehensive Bibliography*. New York: International Universities Press, 1977. [1, 4]

Grollman, E. A. Some signts and insights of history, psychology and psychoanalysis concerning the Father-god and Mother-goddess concepts in Judaism and Christianity. *American Imago*, 1963, *20*, 187-209. [10, 20]

Grollman, E. A. *Judaism in Sigmund Freud's World* (Foreward: Ackerman, N. W.) New York: Block Publishing Company, 1966, xxv + 173 p. [26]

Gross, L. *God and Freud*. New York: McKay, 1957. [38, 39]

de Groot, A. D. *Saint Nicholas: A Psychoanalytic Study of His History and Myth*. New York: Basic Books, 1965. [14]

Grotjahn, M. *The Voice of the Symbol*. Los Angeles: Mara Books, 1971, xv + 224 p. [27]

Grotjahn, M. Psychoanalysis and faith: The thirty-year debate between Sigmund Freud and Oskar Pfister. In S. Post (Ed.) *Moral Values and the Superego Concept in Psychoanalysis*. New York: International Universities Press, 1972. [38]

Groves, E. R. Freudian elements in the animism of the Niger Delta. *The Psychoanalytic Review*, 1917, *4*, 333-338. [6]

Guirdham, A. *Christ and Freud: A Study of Religious Experience and Observance* (Pref: Durrell, L.). London: Allen and Unwin, 1959, 193 p. [38]

Guntrip, H. J. S. *Psychology for Ministers and Social Workers*. London: Independent Press, 1949, 356 p. Chicago: Allenson, 1953. [39]

Guntrip, H. J. S. *Mental Pain and the Cure of Souls* (Foreword, Grensted, L. W.). London: Independent Press, 1956, 206 p. With title: *Psychotherapy and Religion.* New York: Harper, 1957, 206 p. [39]

Guntrip, H. J. S. Psychotherapy and Religion: The constructive use of inner conflict. *Pastoral Psychology*, 1957, *8*, 31-40. [39]

Guntrip, H. J. S. *Personality Structure and Human Interaction*. New York: International Universities Press, 1961. [30, 35]

Guntrip, H. J. S. Religion in relation to personal integration. *British Journal of Medical Psychology*, 1969, *42*, 323-333. [5, 35]

Hacker, F. J. Scientific facts, religious values and the psychoanalytic experience. *Bulletin of the Menninger Clinic,* 1955, *19*, 229-239. [38]

Hacker, F. J. The reality of myth. *International Journal of Psychoanalysis*, 1964, *45*, 438-443. [27]

Halder, A. The Buddhist conception of personality as based

on Abhidharmakosa of Vasubandhu. *Samiksa*, 1967, *21*, 55-56. [9]

Halpern, S. The man who forgot he crucified Jesus: An exegesis of Anatole France's "Procurator of Judea." *The Psychoanalytic Review*, 1964-65, *51*, 597-611. [14]

Held, R. R. Religion, rationalisme et psychanalyse (Religion, rationalism and psychoanalysis). In *Les Cahiers Rationalistes*, Paris: Union Rationaliste, 1959. [5]

Held, R. R. Contribution a l'etude psychanalytique du phenomene religieux (Contribution to the psychoanalytic study of the religious phenomenon). *Revue Francaise de Psychanalyse*, 1962, *26*, 211-266. [5]

Helweg, H. *Soul Sorrow: The Psychiatrist Speaks to the Minister* (Tr. Grano, J.). New York: Pagenat Press, 1955, 151 p. [39]

Herberg, W. Freud, religion and social reality. "The incomprehensible monster, Man." *Commentary*, 1957, *23*, 277-284. [5]

Hesnard, A. L. M. Le Drame de l'aveu (The drama of confession). *Psyche*- Paris, 1949, *4*, 94-104. [39]

Hiltner, S. Case work technique and the therapeutic use of religion. In Tippy, W. M. *Spiritual Factors in Social Work*. Federal Council of the Churches of Christ in America, 1936, 67-70. [39]

Hiltner, S. The contribution of religion to mental health. *Mental Hygiene*, 1940, *24*, 366-377. [39]

Hiltner, S. *Pastoral Counseling*. New York: Abingdon-Cokesbury Press, 1949. [39]

Hiltner, S. Religion and psychoanalysis. *Psychoanalytic Review*, 1950, *37*, 128-139. [5, 38]

Hiltner, S. Pastoral theology and psychology. In Nash, A. S. *Protestant Thought in the Twentieth Century*. New York: Macmillan, 1951, 181-199. [39]

Hiltner, S. Christian faith and psychotherapy. *Religion in Life*, 1952, *2*, 492-501. [39]

Hiltner, S. Some contribution of psychoanalysis to religious understanding. *Complex*, Spring, 1952 (8), 28-40. [38]

Hiltner, S. An appraisal of religion and psychiatry since 1954. *Journal of Religion and Health*, 1965, 4, 217-226. [39]

Hiltner, S. Psychiatry and Religion. *Pastoral Psychology*, 1954, 5, 8-9. [38]

Hiltner, S. Pastoral psychology and pastoral counseling. In Doniger, S. *Religion and Human Behavior.* New York: Association Press, 1954, 179-195. [39]

Hiltner, S. Psychiatry and thoughts on God. *Bulletin of the Menninger Clinic*, 1955, 19, 217-226. [38]

Hiltner, S. Erich Fromm and pastoral psychology. *Pastoral Psychology*, 1955, 6, 11-12. [38]

Hiltner, S. Freud for the pastor. *Pastoral Psychology*, 1955, 5, 41-57. [39]

Hiltner, S. Freud, psychoanalysis and religion. *Pastoral Psychology*, 1956, 7, 9-21. [38]

Hiltner, S. Pastoral care and counseling. *Journal of Religious Thought*, 1956, 13, 111-122. [39]

Hiltner, S. An appraisal of pastoral psychology today. *Pastoral Psychology*, 1957, 6, 9-10. [39]

Hiltner, S. The psychological understanding of religion. In Strunk, O., Jr. (Ed.) *Readings in the Psychology of Religion.* Nashville, Tennessee: Abingdon Press, 1959, 74-104. [5]

Hiltner, S. A program in religion and psychiatry. *Bulletin of the Menninger Clinic*, 1959, 23, 217-225. *Pastoral Psychology*, 1960, 11, 12-18. [39]

Hiltner, S. Psychiatry and Christian hope. *Pastoral Psychology*, 1960, 11, 7-9. [39]

Hiltner, S. The dialogue on man's nature. In Doniger, S. *The Nature of Man.* New York: Harper, 1962, 237-261. [39]

Hiltner, S. Clinical psychology and religion. In Riess, B. and Abt, L. E. (Eds.) *Progress in Clinical Psychology.* New York: Grune and Stratton, 1966, 7, 129-150. [39]

Hiltner, S. and Ziegler, J. H. Clinical pastoral education and the schools. *Journal of Pastoral Care*, 1961, *15*, 129-143. [39]

Hinkle, B. M. The spiritual significance of psychoanalysis. *British Journal of Psychology*, 1921-22, *2*, 209-230. [5, 38]

Hinsie, L. I. Psychoanalysis and heaven. *Psychoanalytic Review*, 1926, *13*, 145-172. [5]

Hitschmann, E. New varieties of religious experience: From William James to Sigmund Freud. In G. Roheim (Ed.) *Psychoanalysis and the Social Sciences*. New York: International Universities Press, 1947. [30]

Hitschmann, E. Swedenborg's paranoia. *American Imago*, 1949, *6*, 45-50. [30]

Holfing, C. K. Notes on Raychaudhuri's "Jesus Christ and Sir Krisna." *American Imago*, 1958, *15*, 213-226. [9, 10]

Homans, P. Toward a psychology of religion by way of Freud and Tillich. *Zygon*, 1967, *2*, 97-119. [5]

Homans, P. *Theology After Freud*. Indianapolis: Bobbs-Merrill, 1970. [5, 12, 38, 39]

Hopkins, P. A critical survey of the psychologies of religion. *Character and Personality*, 1937, *6*, 16-35. [5, 2]

Hopkins, P. Religious beliefs and practices in the land of the Incas. *Religions*, January 1938. [17]

Hora, T. Psychotherapy, existence and religion. *Psychoanalysis and the Psychoanalytic Review*, 1959, *46*, 91-98. [5]

Holand, A. H. "Bosheth" or "Kadesh?" A study into the sources of the obscene ideas about obscenity. *Journal of Sexology and Psychoanalysis*, 1923, *1*, 289-296. [20]

Hsu, F. L. K. *Religion, Science and Human Crises*. London: Routledge and Kegan Paul, 1952, x + 142 p. [38]

Huckel, H. The tragic guilt of Prometheus. *American Imago*, 1955, *12*, 325-336. [18]

Hyman, S. E. The ritual view of myth and mythic. In J. B. Vickery (Ed.) *Myth and Literature: Contemporary Theory and Practice.* Lincoln: University of Nebraska Press, 1966. [27]

Isaacs, K. S., Alexander, J. M. and Haggard, E. A. Faith, trust and gullibility. *International Journal of Psycho-Analysis*, 1963, *44*, 461-469. [31]

Isenberg, M. Morality and the neurotic patient. *American Journal of Psychotherapy*, 1966, *20*, 477-488. [5]

El-Islam, M. F. The psychotherapeutic basis of some Arab rituals. *International Journal of Social Psychiatry*, 1967, *13*, 265-268. [19]

Jacobs, L. I. The primal crime. *Psychoanalytic Review*, 1965, *52*, 456-484. [14, 28]

Jacques, H. P. *Mythologie et Psychanalyse. Le Chatiment de Danaides* (Mythology and Psychoanalysis / The Punishment of the Danaides). Montreal: Les Editions Lemeac, 1969. [18]

Jager-Werth, H. U. Oskar Pfister and the beginnings of religious socialism. *Journal of Religion and Health*, 1974, 57-61. [38]

Jahoda, G. *The Psychology of Superstition.* Baltimore: Penguin Books, 1969, 158 p. [5]

Jekels, L. The psychology of the festival of Christmas. *International Journal of Psychoanalysis*, 1936, *17*, 57-72. [13]

Jones, E. The psychology of religion. *British Journal of Medical Psychology*, 1926, *6*, 264-269. In Jones, E. *Essays in Applied Psychoanalysis.* London, Vienna: International Psychoanalytic Press, 1923. London: The Hogarth Press and the Institute of Psycho-Analysis, 1951, 190-197. [5]

Jones, E. The symbolic significance of salt in folklore and superstition. In Jones, E. *Essays in Applied Psycho-Analysis.* London, Vienna: International Psychoanalytic Press, 1923, 112-203. London: The Hogarth Press and the Institute of Psycho-Analysis, 1951, *2*, 22-109. [5]

Jones, E. The Madonna's conception through the ear - a contribution to the relation between aesthetics and religion.

In author's *Essays in Applied Psycho-Analysis*. London: Vienna: International Psychoanalytic Press, 1923, 261-359. London: The Hogarth Press and the Institute of Psycho-Analysis, 1951, *2*, 266-277. [14]

Jones, E. The God-complex. The belief that one is God and the resulting character traits. In Jones, E. *Essays in Applied Psycho-Analysis*. London, Vienna: International Psychoanalytic Press, 1923, 204-226. London: The Hogarth Press and the Institute of Psycho-Analysis, 1951, *2*, 244-265. [30]

Jones, E. Psychoanalysis and the psychology of religion. In Sandor, L. (Ed.) *Psychoanalysis Today*. New York: Covici-Friede, 1933, 323-337. Under title: The psychology of religion. Sandor, L. (Ed.) *Psychoanalysis Today*. New York: International Universities Press, 1944, 315-325. [5]

Jones, E. A psycho-analytical study of the Holy Ghost. In Jones, E. *Essays in Applied Psycho-Analysis*. London, Vienna: International Psychoanalytic Press, 1923, 415-430. Under title: A Psychoanalytic study of the Holy Ghost Concept. In *Essays in Applied Psychoanalysis*, The Hogarth Press, and the Institute of Psychoanalysis, London, 1951, *2*, 358-373. [14]

Jones, E. *Nightmares, Witches and Devils*. New York: Norton, 1931. [27]

Jones, E. Psychoanalysis and the Christian religion. In Jones, E. *Essays in Applied Psychoanalysis*. London: The Hogarth Press and the Institute of Psychoanalysis, 1951, *2*, 198-211. [10]

Jones, E. The psychology of the Jewish question. In Jones, E. *Essays in Applied Psycho-Analysis*. London, Vienna: International Psychoanalytic Press. London: The Hogarth Press and the Institute of Psycho-Analysis, 1951, *1*, 284-300. [20]

Jones, E. *Essays in Applied Psychoanalysis. Vol. II. Essays in Folklore, Anthropology and Religion*. London: Hogarth Press, 1951. [5]

Jones, E. *The Life and Work of Sigmund Freud. 3 Vols.* New York: Basic Books, 1953. [4]

Jones, E. The inception of *Totem and Taboo. International Journal of Psychoanalysis*, 1956, *37*, 34-35. [28]

Jones, E. The birth and death of Moses. *International Journal of Psychoanalysis*, 1958, *39*, 1-4. [20]

Jones, I. H. Subincision among Australian western desert aborigines. *British Journal of Medical Psychology*, 1969, *42*, 183-190. [32]

Jones, A. The original sin of mankind: An attempt at a psychological interpretation. In Belgum, D. *Religion and Medicine.* Ames: Iowa State University Press, 1967, 135-143. [38]

Kamiat, A. H. Further remarks on the believer's delusion of infallibility. *Psychoanalytic Review*, 1926, *13*, 309-311. [31]

Kamiat, A. H. A psychology of asceticism. *Journal of Abnormal and Social Psychology*, 1928, *23*, 223-232. [30]

Kamiat, A. H. The cosmic phantasy. *Psychoanalytic Review*, 1928, *15*, 210-219. [5]

Kaplan, A. Maturity in religion. *Bulletin of the Philadelphia Association for Psychoanalysis.* 1963, *13*, 101-119. [38]

Kaplan, B. Psychological themes in Zuni mythology and Zuni TAT's *Psychoanalytic Study of Society*, 1962, *2*, 255-262. [7, 27]

Kaplan, L. The Baalschem legend (Tr. Green, Z.) *Psyche and Eros*, 1921, *2*, 173-183.

Kaplan, L. The belief in witches and in magic (A psychoanalytic study). *Journal of Sexology and Psychoanalysis.* 1923, *1*, 349-363. [5]

Karlson, K. J. Psychoanalysis and mythology. *Journal of Religious Psychology*, 1914, 7, 137-213. [27]

Katz, J. The Joseph dream anew. *Psychoanalytic Review*, 1963, *50*, 252-278. [24]

Katz, R. L. A psychoanalytic comment on Job 3.25. *Hebrew Union College Annual*, 1958, *29*, 377-383. [24]

Kaufman, M. R. Religious delusions in schizophrenia. *International *Journal of Psycho-Analysis*, 1939, *20*, 363-376. [30]

Kelman, H. Communing and relating. Part I. Past and current perspectives. *American Journal of Psychoanalysis* 1958, *18*, 77-98. [9]

Kew, C. E. and Kew, C. J. Principles and values of group psychotherapy under church auspices. *Pastoral Psychology*, 1955, *6*, 37-48. [39]

Kew, C. E., and Kew, C. J. Writing as an aid in pastoral counseling and psychotherapy. *Pastoral Psychology*, 1963, *14*, 37-43. [39]

Kiell, Norman. *Psychoalaysis, Psychology and Literature: A Bibliography*. Madison: The University of Wisconsin Press, 1963. [1]

Kiev, A. Ritual goat sacrifice in Haiti. *American Imago*, 1962, *19*, 349-359. [33]

Kiev, A. Primitive religious rites and behavior: Clinical considerations. *International Psychiatry Clinics*, 1969, *5*, 119-131. [5, 17]

Klauber, J. The present status of Freud's views of religion. *Synagogue Review*, 1960, *34*, 219-225. [5]

Klauber, J. Notes on the psychical roots of religion, with particular reference to the development of Western Christianity. *International Journal of Psychoanalysis*, 1974, *55*, 249-255. [10, 28]

Klausner, S. Z. Sacred and profane meanings of blood and alcohol. *Journal of Social Psychology*, 1964, *64*. 27-43. [5, 37]

Klein, M. *Contributions to Psychoanalysis, 1921-1945*. London: Hogarth Press, 1965. [30, 35]

Kleinschmidt, H. J. Beyond Philip Rieff: The triumph of Sigmund Freud. *American Imago*, 1966, *23*, 244-256. [5]

Klibansky, R., Panofsky, E. and Saxl, F. *Saturn and Melancholy. Studies in the History of Natural Philosophy, Religion, and Art*. New York: Basis Books, 1964, 429 p. [5]

Kligerman, C. A psychoanalytic study of the confessions of St. Augustine. *Journal of the American Psychoanalytic Association*, 1957, *5*, 469-484. [30]

Kluckhohn, C. Myths and rituals: A general theory. *Harvard Theological Review*, 1942, *35*, 45-79. [27]

Kluckhohn, C. Recurrent themes in myths and myth-making. *Daedalus*, 1959, *88*, 268-279. [27]

Knight, J. The use and misuse of religion by the emotionally disturbed. *Pastoral Psychology*, 1962, *13*, 10-18. [39]

Knight, J. A Calvinism and psychoanalysis: A comparative study. *Pastoral Psychology*, 1963, *14*, 10-17. [38]

Knight, J. A. *A Psychiatrist Looks at Religion and Health.* New York: Ashville: Abingdon Press, 1964, 207 p. [38]

Knight, J. A. Partners in healing. *Pulpit Digest*, 1964, October, 11-18. [39]

Knight, J. A. Religious-psychological conflicts of the adolescent. In Usdin, G. L. *Adolescence.* Philadelphia: Lippincott, 1967, 31-50. [38]

Knight, J. A. Church phobia. *Pastoral Psychology*, 1967, *18*, 33-38. [39]

Knight, J. A. Adolescent development and religious values. *Voices*, 1969, *4*, 68-72. [38]

Knight, R. P. Practical and theoretical considerations in the analysis of a minister. *Psychoanalytic Review*, 1937, *24*, 350-364. [30]

Kohen, M. The Venus of Willendorf. *American Imago*, 1946, *3*, 49-60. [29]

Kondo, A. Intuition in Zen Buddhism. *American Journal of Psychoanalysis*, 1952, *12*, 10-14. [9]

Krapf, E. E. Shylock and Antonio: A psychoanalytic study of Shakespeare and anti-semitism. *Psychoanalytic Review*, 1955, *42*, 113-130. [20]

Kraus, R. F. A psychoanalytic interpretation of shamanism. *Psychoanalytic Review*, 1972, *59*, 19-32. [17]

Kristol, I. God and the psychoanalyst. *Commentary*, 1949,

*8*, 434-443. [5]

Kroeber, A. L. Totem and Taboo. *American Anthropologist*, 1920, *22*, 48-55. [28]

Kroeber, A. L. "Totem and Taboo" in retrospect. *American Journal of Sociology*, 1939, *45*, 446-451. [28]

Kupper, H. I. Psychodynamics of the intellectual. *International Journal of Psycho-Analysis*, 1949, *30*, 201-202; 1950, *31*, 85-94. [31]

La Barre, W. A cultist drug-addiction in an Indian alcoholic. *Bulletin of the Menninger Clinic*, 1941, *5*, 40-46. [7]

La Barre, W. Primitive psychotherapy in native American cultures: Peyotism and confession. *Journal of Abnormal and Social Psychology*, 1947, *42*, 294-309. [7]

La Barre, W. The influence of Freud on anthropology. *American Imago*, 1958, *15*, 276-328. [5]

La Barre, W. Religions, Rorschachs and tranquilizers. *American Journal of Orthopsychiatry*, 1959, *29*, 688-698. [5]

La Barre, W. *The Human Animal*, Chicago: University of Chicago Press, 1959. [5]

La Barre, W. *They Shall Take Up Serpents*, Minneapolis: University of Minnesota Press, 1962. [16, 32]

La Barre, W. Confession as cathartic therapy in native American Indian tribes. In A. Kiev (Ed.) *Magic, Faith, and Healing*. New York: Free Press, 1964. [7]

La Barre, W. *The Peyote Cult*. 2nd Ed. New York: Schocken Books, 1969. [7]

La Barre, W. *The Ghost Dance: The Origins of Religion*. New York: Doubleday, 1970. [5, 28]

Laforgue, R. La pensee magique dans la religion (Magic thought in religion). *Revue Franciase de Psychanalyse*, 1934, 7, 19-31. [31]

Laforgue, R. La foi et l'equilibre psychique de l'homme (Faith and the psychic equilibrium of man). *Psyche* (Paris), 1953, 8, 305-323. [39]

Laguna, F. de Method and theory of ethnology. In author's

*American Anthropologist: Selected Papers, 1888-1920.* Evanston, Illinois: Row, Peterson, 1960, 782-792. [5]

Larsen, L. and Knapp, R. H. Sex differences in symbolic conceptions of the deity. *Journal of Projective Techniques and Personality Assessment*, 1964, *28*, 303-306. [37]

Lawton, G. The psychology of spiritualist mediums. *Psychoanalytic Review*, 1932, *19*, 418-445. [33]

Leach, Edmund R. Pulleyar and the Lord Buddha: An aspect of religious syncretism in Ceylon. *Psychoanalysis and the Psychoanalytic Review*, 1962, *48*, 81-102. [9]

Leach, E. R. (Ed.) *The Structural Study of Myth and Totemism.* London: Tavistock, 1967, 185 p. [27]

Leavy, S. A. A religious conversion in a four-year-old girl: A historical note. *Bulletin of the Philadelphia Association for Psychoanalysis*, 1957, *7*, 85-90. [10, 31]

Leavy, S. A. The psychic function of religion in mental illness and health. *Group for the Advancement of Psychiatry Reports*, 1968, *67*, 647-730. [38]

Lederer, W. Dragons, delinquents, and destiny: An essay on positive superego functions. *Psychological Issues, No. 15.* New York: International Uiversitites Press, 1964. [5]

Lederer, W. Oedipus and the serpent. *The Psychoanalytic Review*, 1964-65, *51*, 619-644. [8, 18, 20]

Lederer, W. Historical consequences of father-son hostility. *The Psychoanalytic Review*, 1967, *54*, 248-276. [18, 20]

Lee, R. S. *Freud and Christianity.* New York: A. A. Wyn, 1949, 204 p. [38]

Lehrman, S. R. Psychopathology in mixed marriages. *The Psychoanalytic Quarterly*, 1967, *36*, 67-82. [31]

Leighton, A. H. and Leighton, D. C. Elements of psychotherapy in Navaho religion. *Psychiatry*, 1941, *4*, 515-523. [7]

Lemercier, G. Freud in the cloister: Interview. *Atlas*, 1967, *13*, 33-37. [38]

Lepp, I. *The Depths of the Soul: A Christian Approach to*

*Psychoanalysis*. Staten Island, New York: Alba House, 1966, 280 p. Garden City, New York: Image Books, 1967, 274 p. [38]

Lesser, G. S. Religion and the defensive responses in children's fantasy. *Journal of Projective Techniques*, 1959, *23*, 64-68. [37]

Leschnitzer, A. F. Faust and Moses. *American Imago*, 1949, *6*, 229-243. [24]

Leverenz, D. Shared fantasy in Puritan sermons. *American Imago*, 1975, *32*, 264-287. [10]

Levin, A. J. Oedipus and Samson, the rejected hero-child. *International Journal Of Psychoanalysis*, 1957, *38*, 105-116. [24, 27]

Levin, T. M. and Zegans, L. S. Adolescent identity crisis and religious conversion: Implications for psychotherapy. *British Journal of Medical Psychology*, 1974, *47*, 73-82. [30]

Lewis, T. N. Freud, the Jew and Judaism. *Jewish Spectator.* New York, 1958, March, 11-14. [26]

Lidz, R., Lidz, T. and Barton-Bradley, B. G. Cargo cultism: A psychosocial study of Melanesian millenarianism. *Journal of Nervous and Mental Disease*, 1973, *157*, 370-388. [33]

Lidz, T. and Rothenberg, A. Psychedelism:Dyonysus reborn. *Psychiatry*, 1968, *31*, 116-125. [10, 18]

Linn, L. On the difference between psychiatry and religion. In Noveck, S. *Judaism and Psychiatry*. New York: Basic Books, 1956.

Linn, L. The boundary line between psychiatry and religion. In Noveck, S. (Ed.) *Judaism and Psychiatry*, 177-181. [38]

Linn, L. The need to beieve. In Noveck, S. *Judaism and Psychiatry*, 129-134. [38]

Linn, L. and Schwarz, L. W. *Psychiatry and Religious Experience*. New York: Random House, 1958, 307 p. [38]

Locke, N. A myth of ancient Egypt. *American Imago*, 1961, *18*, 105-128. [8]

Lodge, A. Satan's symbolic sundrome: A psychological interpretation of Milton's Satan. *Psychoanalytic Review*,

1956, *43*, 411-422. [14]

Loeblowitz-Lennard, H. A psychoanalytic contribution to the problem of anti-semitism. *Psychoanalytic Review*, 1945, *32*, 359-361. [20]

Loeblowitz-Lennard, H. The Jew as symbol. I. The ritual murder myth. *Psychoanalytic Quarterly*, 1947, *16*, 33-38. [20]

Loeblowitz-Lennard, H. The Jew as symbol. II. Anti-Semitism and transference. *Psychiatric Quarterly*, 1947, *21*, 253-260. [20]

Loewenberg, P. Sigmund Freud as a Jew: A study in ambivalence and courage. *Journal of the History of the Behavioral Sciences*, 1972, *7*, 363-369. [26]

Loewenstein, R. M. The historical and cultural roots of anti-Semitism. In *Psychoanalysis and the Social Sciences*, 1947, *1*, 313-356. [20]

Loewenstein, R. M. *Christians and Jews*. New York: International Universities Press, 1951. [10, 20]

Lombillo, J. R. The soldier saint - a psychological analysis of the conversion of Ignatius of Loyola. *Psychiatric Quarterly*, 1973, *47*, 386-418. [30]

Loomis, E. A., Jr. Psychiatry and the Christian ministry. *Union Theological Seminary Quarterly Review*, 1957, *12*, 31-39. [39]

Loomis, E. A., Jr. *The Self in Pilgrimage*, New York: Harper, 1960, xvii + 104 p. [38]

Loomis, E. A., Jr. Religion and psychiatry. In Deutsch, A. and Fishman, H. (Eds.) *The Encyclopedia of Mental Health*. New York: Franklin Watts, 1963, 1965, 1748-1759. [39]

Lopez Ibor, J. J. Angoisse vecue et vocation religieuse (Experience of anxiety and religious vocation). *Psyche* - (Paris), 1954, *9*, 433-446. [39]

Lorand, S. Dream interpretation in the Talmlud. *International Journal of Psychoanalysis*, 1957, *38*, 92-97. [20]

Lorand, S. Psycho-analytic therapy of religious devotees (A

theoretical and technical contribution). *The International Journal of Psycho-Analysis*, 1962, *43*, 50-56. [31]

Lourie, A. The Jewish God and the Greek hero. *American Imago*, 1948, *5*, 152-166. [18, 20]

Lourie, A. The Jew as a psychological type. *American Imago*, 1949, *6*, 119-155. [20]

Lowenfeld, H. The decline in belief in the devil: The consequence for group psychology. *The Psychoanalytic Quarterly*, 1969, *38*, 455-462. [12]

Lowtzky, F. Soeren Kierkegaard: l'experience subjective et la revelation religieuse. Etude psychanalytique. *Revue Francaise de Psychanalyse*, 1936, *9*, 204-315. [30]

Lubin, A. J. A feminine Moses: A bridge between childhood identifications and adult identity. *International Journal of Psychoanalysis*, 1958, *39*, 535-546. [30]

Lubin, A. J. A boy's view of Jesus. In R. S. Eissler et al. (Eds.) *The Psychoanalytic Study of the Child*, 1959, *3*, 155-168. [31]

Lubin, A. J. The influence of the Russian Orthodox Church on Freud's Wolf-Man: A hypothesis (with an epilogue based on visits with the Wolf-Man). *The Psychoanalytic Forum*, 1967, *2*, 146-162, 170-174. [30]

Lubin, A. J. A psychoanalytic view of religion. In E. M. Pattison (Ed.) *Clinical Psychiatry and Religion*. Boston: Little, Brown & Co., 1969. [5, 38]

Lubin, M. Study of the high rate of male Jewish membership in the profession of psychoanalysis. *Proceedings of the 77th Annual Convention of the American Psychological Association*, 1969, *4*, 527-528. [26]

Lussheimer, P. Psychoanalysis and religion. *American Journal of Psychoanalysis*, 1953, *18*, 88, [5]

Lustig, E. On the origins of Judaism: A psycoanalytic approach. *The Psychoanalytic Study of Society*, 1976, *7*, 359-367. [20]

Maguire, J. D. Theological uses of psychoanalysis: Patterns problems, and proposals. *Religion in Life*, 1962, *31*, 169-184. [38]

Mailloux, N. Obstacles to the realization of the ascetic ideal. In *Christian Asceticism and Modern Man.* New York: Philo Library, 1955, 237-252. [38]

Mailloux, N. Psychology and spiritual direction. In Braceland, F. J. *Faith, Reason and Modern Psychiatry*, New York: Kennedy, 1955, 247-263. [38]

Mailloux, N. Religious and moral issues in psychotherapy and counseling. *Ann New York Academy of Science*, 1955, *63*, 427-428. [38]

Maler, M. The Jewish Orthodox circumcision ceremony: Its meaning from direct study of the rite. *Journal of the American Psychoanalytic Association*, 1966, *14*, 510-517.

Malev, M. The value of ritual. In Noveck, S. *Judaism and Psychiatry*, 135-142. New York: Random House, 1956. [38]

Malev, M. Discussion of the paper by John Klauber on "Psychical roots of religion." *Internaional Journal of Psychoanalysis*, 1974, *55*, 257-259. [28]

Malony, N. H. and North, G. The future of an illusion and the illusion of a future. *Journal of the History of the Behavioral Sciences*, in press. [38]

Mann, J. (Reporter) Panel on clinical and theoretical aspects of religious belief (Read at Am Psa Ass, May 1963). *Journal of the American Psychoanalytic Association*, 1964, *12*, 160-170. [5]

Mannoni, O. *Freud*, New York: Pantheon, 1971. [5]

Marcus, N. N. Prometheus reconsidered. *Psychoanalytic Review*, 1967, *54*, 83-107. [18]

Marmorston, J. and Stainbrook, E. (Eds.) *Psychoanalysis and the Human Situation*, New York / Washington / Hollywood: Vantage Press, 1964, 270 p. [5]

Masih, Y. *Freudianism and Religion.* Calcutta: Thacker Spink, 1964, 356 p. [5]

May, R. Forward to Guntrip, H., *Psychotherapy and Religion*, 7-10. [39]

May, R. Religious psychotherapy and achievement of selfhood. *Pastoral Psychology*, 1951, *2*, 15-20, *2*, 26-35. [39]

McClelland, D. C. *Psychoanalysis and Religious Mysticism*, Wallingford, Pa.: Pendle Hill, 1959, 32 p. [31]

McClelland, D. C. *The Roots of Consciousness*. Princeton, N. J.: Van Nostrand, 1964, v + 219 p. [5]

McLeish, J. Psychoanalytic imperialism: Freudian methodology and primitive religion. *Dublin Review*, 1960, *234*, 227-238. [28]

McNeill, H. V. Freudians and Catholics. *The Commonwealth*, 1947, *46*, 350-353. [38]

Meadow, A. and Vetter, H. J. Freudian theory and the Judaic value system. *International Journal of Social Psychiatry*, 1959, *5*, 197-207. [26]

Medlicott, R. W. St. Anthony Abbot and the hazards of asceticism: An analysis of artists' representations of the temptations. *British Journal of Medical Psychology* 1969, *42*, 133-140. [30]

Medlicott, R. W. Leda and the swan - An analysis of the theme in myth and art. *Australian and New Zealand Journal of Psychiatry*, 1970, *4*, 15-23. [18]

Meissner, W. W. *Annotated Bibliography in Religion and Psychology*. New York: The Academy of Religion and Mental Health, 1961. [1]

Meng, H. and Freud, E. L. (Eds.) *Psychoanalysis and Faith: The Letters of Sigmund Freud and Oskar Pfister*, New York: Basic Books, 1963. [4]

Menninger, K. A. Psychiatry looks at religion. In author.s *A Psychiatrist's World: Selected Papers*, 793-802. [38]

Menninger, K. A. The genius of the Jew in psychiatry. *Medical Leaves*, 1937, *1*, 127-132. [26]

Menninger, K. Psychoanalysis and the ministry. *Pastoral Psychology*, 1958, *9*, 59, [39]

Menninger, K. and Pruyser, P. W. Religious and spiritual values. In Doniger, S. *Becoming the Complete Adult*. New York: Associated Press, 1962, 95-118. [39]

Meyerhoff, H. By love redeemed. A fantasy on "God and Freud." *Commentary*, 1959, *2*, 202-206. [38]

Meyerson, O. G. and Stoller, L. A psychoanalytic interpretation of the crucifixion. *Psychoanalysis and the Psychoanalytic Review*, 1962, *49*, 117-118. [38]

Miller, S. H. Exploring the boundary between religion and psychiatry. *Journal of Pastoral Care*, 1952, *6*, 1-11. [39]

Milner, M. The sense in non-sense (Freud and Blake's "Job"). *New Era*, London, 1956, *7*, 29-41. [31]

Misch, R. C. Impulse control and social feeling. *International Psychiatry Clinics*, 1966, *3*, 117-137. [31]

Miura, T. Psychoanalysis and religion. *The Japanese Journal of Psycho-Analysis*, 1955, *2*, 5-10. [5]

Mollegen, A. T. A Christian view of psychoanalysis. In *Christianity and Psychoanalysis*. Washington: Organizing Committee, Christianity and Modern Man, 1952, 1 - 18. [38]

Mollegen, A. F. Utilization of religious attitudes in clinical psychiatry. *Bulletin of Isaac Ray Medical Library*, 1954, *2, 116-135. [39]*

Moller, H. Affective mysticism in Western civilization. *The psychoanalytic Review*, 1965, *52*, 259-274. [31]

Moloney, J. C. Mother, God and superego. *Journal of the American Psychoanalytic Association*, 1954, *2*, 120-151. [5]

Moloney, J. C. Carnal myths involving the sun. *American Imago*, 1963, *20*, 93-104. [8, 27]

de Monchy, S. J. R. Adam - Cain - Oedipus. *American Imago*, 1962, *19*, 3-17. [24, 28]

Money-Kryle, R. E. *The Meaning of Sacrifice*, London: The Hogarth Press and the Institute of Psycho-Analysis, 1930, 273 p. [32]

Money-Kryle, R. E. *Religion in a Changing World*. London: Watts and Company: The Rationalist Annual, 1948. [5]

Moore, T. V. Religion, psychiatry, and mental hygiene. *Psychiatry*, 1944, *7*, 321-326. [38]

Mora, G. The scrupulosity syndrome. *International Psychiatric Clinics*, 1969, *5*, 163-174. [30]

More, J. The prophet Jonah: The story of an intrapsychic process. *American Imago*, 1970, *27*, 3-11. [24]

Mowrer, O. H. The unocnscious re-examined in a religious context. In Strunk, O. Jr. (Ed.) *Readings in the Psychology of Religion*. Nashville, Tennessee: Abingdon Press, 1959. [38]

Mowrer, O. H. Psychopathology and the problem of guilt, confession, and expiation. In Dennis, W. et al. *Current Trends in Psychological Theory*. Pittsburgh: University of Pittsburgh Press, 1961, 208 - 229. [38]

Mowrer, O. H. Sigmund Freud: Psychopathologist or "theologian." *Psychiatry Digest*, 1965, *26*, 39-47. [38]

Moxon, C. Religion in the light of psycho-analysis. *Psychoanalytic Review*, 1921, *8*, 92-98. [5]

Moxon, C. Epileptic traits in Paul of Tarsus. *Psychoanalytic Review*, 1922, *9*, 60-66. [30]

Moxon, C. *Freudian Essays in Religion and Science*. Boston: Badger, 1927. [5]

Moxon, C. A psychoanalytic study of the Christian creed. *International Journal of Psychoanalysis*, 1931, *2*, 54-70. [12]

Moxon, C. Freud's denial of religion. *British Journal of Medical Psychology*, 1931, *11*, 150-157. [5]

Muensterberger, W. Remarks on the function of mythology. *The Psychoanalytic Study of Society*, 1964, *3*, 94-97. [27]

Muensterberger, W. (Ed.) *Man and His Culture: Psychoanalytic Anthropology After "Totem and Taboo."* New York: Toplinger Publishing Company, 1970. [28]

Murphy, G. Religion and the social sciences. *Religion* (Kansas), 1968, *5*, 1-4. [38]

Murray, H. A. (Ed.) *Myth and Mythemaking*. New York: Braziller, 1960, 381 p. [27]

Naftalin, M, Footnote to the genesis of Moses. *The Psychoanalytic Quarterly*, 1958, *27*, 402-405. [24]

Natterson, J. M. Jewishness as resistance. *The Psychoanalytic Review*, 1966, *53*, 94-98. [20]

Namburg, M. Religious symbols in the unconscious of man. *International Record of Medicine*, 1958, *17*, 723-731. [5]

Nelson, B. B. The future of illusions. *Psychoanalysis*, 1951, *2*, 16-37. [5]

Nelson, M. O. The concept of God and feelings towards parents. *Journal of Individual Psychology*, 1971, *27*, 46-49. [37]

Nelson, M. O. and Jones, E. M. An application of the Q-technique to the study of religious concepts. *Psychological Reports*, 1957, *3*, 293-297. [37]

Neu, J. Genetic explanation in Totem and Taboo. In R. Wolheim (Ed.) *Freud*. Garden City, New York: Doubleday, 1974. [27]

Newell, H. W. An interpretation of the Hindu worship of Siva Linga. *Bulletin of the Philadelphia Association for Psychoanalysis*, 1954, *4*, 82-86. [9]

Niebur, U. M. "Sex in Christianity and Psychoanalysis." *Religion in Life*, 1956, *25*, 613-618. [39]

Niederland, W. G. Jacob's dream: with some remarks on ladder and river symbolism. *Journal of Hillside Hospital*, 1954, *3*, 73-97. [24]

Nodet, C. H. Considerations psychoanalytiques a propos des attraits neurotiques pour la vie religieuse (Psychoanalytic considerations regarding neurotic attractions to the religious life). *Supplement de la Vie Spirituelle*, 1954, *28*, 53-63. [39]

Noveck, S. *Judaism and Psychiatry: Two Approaches to the Personal Problems and Needs of Modern Man*. New York: Basic Books, 1956, xiii + 197 p. [38]

Novey, S. Considerations on religion in relation to psychoanalysis and psychotherapy. *Journal of Nervous and Mental Diseases*, 1960, *130*, 315-324. [30]

Nunberg, H. *Problems of bisexuality as reflected in circumcision*. London: Imago Publishing, 1949. [25]

Oates, W. *The Christian Pastor*. Philadelphia: Westminster Press, 1951. [39]

O'Doherty, E. F. Toward a dynamic psychology: Freud and St. Thomas. *Studies*, 1960, *49*, 341-354. [38]

Oehschlegel, L. Regarding Freud's book on Moses: A religio-psychoanalytical study. *The Psychoanalytic Review*, 1943, *30*, 67-77. [24, 26]

Ostow, M. Biological basis of religious symbolism. *International Record of Medicine*, 1958, *171*, 709-717. [5]

Ostow, M. The nature of religious controls. *American Psychologicst*, 1958, *13*, 571-574. [5]

Ostow, M. Religion and psychoanalysis: The area of common concern. *Pastoral Psychology*, 1959, *19*, 33-38. [38]

Ostow, M. Religion. In Arieti, S. (Ed.) *American Handbook of Psychiatry*. New York: Basic Books, 1966, II, 1789-1801. [5]

Ostow, M. Religion and morality: A psychoanalytic view. In S. Post (Ed.) *Moral Values and the Superego Concept in Psychoanalysis*, New York: International Universities Press, 1972. [38]

Outler, A. C. *Psychotherapy and the Christian Message*. New York: Harper, 1954. [39]

Oyama, J. Comparative study on the psychoanalysis and Buddhism theory. *Sendai Journal of Psychoanalysis*, 1953, 4-5. [9]

Oyama, J. Consideration of mental conflict and Adana-Vijnana. *Sendai Journal of Psychoanalysis*, 1953, *18-20*. [9]

Oyama, J. Psycho-analysis of religious exaltation. *The Japanese Journal of Psycho-Analysis*, 1957, *4*, 1-9. [31]

Oyama, J. The theories of personality in psychoanalysis and the concept of the Three Consciousnesses (Vijnana) in Buddhism I. On Es and manovijanana. *American Journal of Psychoanalysis*, 1958, *5*, 9-14. [9]

Paddock, F. A philosophical investigation of the relation between psychoanalysis and theology. *Journal of Pastoral Care*, 1959, *13*, 38-41. [38]

Palm, R. On the symbolic significance of the Star of David. *American Imago*, 1958, *15*, 227-231. [21]

Panel. Mythology and ego psychology. *The Psychoanalytic Study of Society*, 1964, *3*, 4-87. [27, 34]

Parcells, F. H. and Segel, N. P. Oedipus and the Prodigal Son. *Psychoanalytic Quarterly*, 1959, *28*, 213-227. [14]

Parrot, P. and Romain, R. P. Maturite affective et vocation sacerdotale (Affective maturity and the vocation of priesthood.) *Supplement de la Vie Spirituelle*, 1958, *46*, 307-322. [39]

Pasche, F. Freud et l'orthodoxie judeo-chretienne (Freud and Judeo-Christian orthodoxy). *Revue Francaise de Psychanalyse*, 1961. *25*, 55-87. [5]

Pasquarelli, B. Psychoanalysis and religion - a postulated autonomy in function. *Bulletin of the Philadelphia Association for Psychoanalysis*, 1960, *10*, 10-17. [38]

Pattison, E. M. On the failure to forgive or to be forgiven. *American Journal of Psychotherapy*, 1965, *19*, 106-115. [39]

Pattison, E. M. (Ed.) *Clinical Psychiatry and Religion*. International Psychiatry Clinics, Vol. 5 (4). Boston: Little, Brown, 1969, xii + 327 p. [38]

Paul, R. A. The Sherpa temple as a model of the psyche. *American Ethnologist*, 1976, *3*, 131-146. [9]

Paul, R. A. Did the primal crime take place? *Ethos*, 1976, *4*, 311-352. [5]

Paul, R. A. The eyes outnumber the nose two to one. *Psychoanalytic Review*, in press. [9]

Paul, R. A. A mantra and its meaning. *The Psychoanalytic Study of Society*, in press. [9]

Pearson, G. H. J. A note on the medusa: A speculative attempt to explain a ritual. *Bulletin of the Philadelphia Association for Psychoanalysis*, 1967, *17*, 1-9. [8, 18, 29]

Pederson, S. Unconscious motives in pro-semitic attitudes. *Psychoanalytic Review*, 1951, *38*, 361-373. [20]

Peto, A. The demonic mother image in the Jewish religion. *Psychoanalysis and the Social Sciences*, 1958, *5*, 280-287. [24]

Peto, A. The development of ethical monotheism. *The Psychoanalytic Study of Society*, 1960, *1*, 311-375. [20]

Philp, H. L. *Freud and Religious Belief*. London: Rockliff, 1956. [5]

Phipott, S. J. F. Unconscious mechanisms in religion. *British Journal of Medical Psychology*, 1942, *19*, 292-312. [5]

Ple, A. St. Thomas and the psychology of Freud. In Birmingham, W. and Cunneen, J. E. (Eds.) *Cross Currents of Psychiatry And Catholic Morality*. New York: Pantheon Books, 1964, 84 - 109. [38]

Pollock, R. E. Some psychoanalytic considerations of bull fighting and bull worship. *Israel Annals of Psychiatry and Related Disciplines*, 1974, *12*, 53-67. [8]

Posinsky, S. H. Ritual, neurotic and social. *American Imago*, 1962, *19*, 375-390. [32]

Postle, B. Religion in the psychologies of Jung and Freud. *Ohio State Medical Journal*, 1947, *43*, 947-950. [5]

Prince, R. The Yoruba image of the witch. *British Journal of Psychiatry*, 1961, *107*, 795-805. [6]

Prince, R. Indigenous Yoruba Psychiatry. In Kiev, A. *Magic, Faith and Healing*. Glencoe, Illinois: Free Press. London: Collier-Macmillan, 1964, 84-120. [6]

Prince, R. Fundamental differences of psychoanalysis and faith healing. *International Journal of Psychiatry*, 1972, *10*, 125-128. [31, 38]

Prince, R. and Savage, C. Mystical States and the Concept of regression. *Psychedelic Review*, 1966, *8*, 59-75. [31]

Proust, M. Freud et Saint Paul (Freud and St. Paul). *Psyche - Paris*, 1947, *2*, 464-467. [38]

Pruyser, P. W. *A Dynamic Psychology of Religion*. New York: Harper and Row, 1968. [5]

Pruyser, P. W. Sigmund Freud and his legacy: Psychoanalytic psychology of religion. In C. Y. Glock and P. E. Hammond (Eds.) *Beyond the Classics? Essays in the Scientific Study of Religion*. New York: Harper and Row, 1973. [4, 5]

Putnam, J. J. The service to nervous invalids of the physician and the minister. *Harvard Theological Review*, 1909, April 1. [39]

Racker, E. (Heinrich) On Freud's position towards religion. *American Imago*, 1956, *13*, 97-121. [5]

Ramnoux, C. La fete du premier Novembre (The Holiday of the first of November, the "All Saints" Day). *Psyche* - Paris, 1948, *3*, 1020 - 1040. [13]

Ramnoux, C. Sur une page de "Moise et le monotheisme" (About a page from "Moses and monotheism"). *Psychanalyse*, 1957, *3*, 165-187. [20]

Rank, O. *The Myth of the Birth of the Hero: A Psychological Interpretation of Mythology*. Nervous and Mental Diseases Monograph Series 18. New York: Nervous and Mental Diseases Publishing Company, 1914, iii + 100 p. [27]

Rank, O. and Sachs, H. The significance of psychoanalysis for the humanities. *American Imago*, 1964, *21*, 7-128. [5]

Redl, F. Fritz Redl on "Den Heiligen Nikolaus." In Groot, A. de, *Saint Nicholas, A Psychoanalytic Study*. Hague: Mouton, 1965. [14]

Reid, R. E. Infantile crises associated with Christmas: A psychoanalytic interpretation. *Dissertation Abstracts*, 1968, *29*, (1-A), 321. [13]

Reider, N. Chess, Oedipus and the Mater Dolorosa. *International Journal of Psycho-Analysis*, 1959, *40*, 515-528. [8, 10]

Reider, N. Medieval Oedipal legends about Judas. *Psychoanalytic Quarterly*, 1960, *29*, 515-527. [14]

Reik, T. Mythology (Collected Reviews). *International Journal of Psycho-Analysis*, 1921, *2*, 101-105. [2, 27]

Reik T. The therapy of the neuroses and religion. *International Journal of Psycho-Analysis*, 1929, *10*, 292-302. [5]

Reik, T. *Ritual: Psycho-Analytic Studies.* New York: Norton, 1931, 367 p. With title: *The Psychological Problems of Religion.* New York: Farrar, Straus, 1946. [32]

Reik, T. Puberty rites among savages. On some similarities in the mental life of savages and neurotics. In author's *Ritual: Psychoanalytic Studies*, 91-166. [32]

Reik, T. The Shofar (Ram's Horn). In author's *Ritual: Psychoanalytic Studies*, 221-361. [21]

Reik, T. *Dogma and Compulsion*. New York: International Universities Press, 1951. [12, 24, 25, 36]

Reik, T. Man the mythmaker. In Reik, T. *Dogma and Compulsion*. New York: International Universities Press, 1951. [27]

Reik, T. The prayer shawl and phylacterics of the Jews: A psychoanalytic contribution to Hebrew archeology. In author's *Dogma and Compulsion: Psychoanalytic Studies of Myths of Religions*, 181-228. [21]

Reik, T. Psychoanalytic Studies of Bible Exegesis I. The wrestling of Jacob. In author's *Dogma and Compulsion: Psychoanalytic Studies of Myth and Religions*, 229-275. [24]

Reik, T. Freud and Jewish Wit. *Psychoanalysis, Journal of the National Psychological Association for Psychoanalysis*, 1954, *2*, 12-20. [26]

Reik, T. From spell to prayer. *Psychoanalysis*, 1955, *3*, (1), 3-26. [32]

Reik, T. The face of God. *Psychoanalysis*, 1955, *3*, (2), 3-26. [22, 36]

Reik, T. *Myth and Guilt*. New York: Braziller, 1957. [24]

Reik, T. *Mystery of the Mountain: The Drama of the Sinai Revelation*. New York: Harper, 1959, xiii + 210 p. [24]

Reik, T. *The Creation of Woman: A Psychoanalytic Inquiry into the Myth of Eve*. New York: G. Braziller, 1960, viii + 159 p. [24]

Reik, T. *The Temptation*. New York: Braziller, 1961, 256 p. [24]

Reik, T. A booth away from the house. *The Psychoanalytic Review*, 1963, *50*, 167-186. [23, 25]

Reik, T. *Pagan Rites in Judaism*. New York: Farrar, Straus, 1964, 206 p. [23, 25, 36]

Reiser, O. L. The biological origins of religion. *The Psychoanalytic Review*, 1932, *19*, 1-22. [28]

Ricketts, M. L. Anthropological psychoanalysis of religion, *History of Religions*, 1971, *11*, 147-156. [5]

Ricoeur, P. *Freud and Philosophy: An Essay on Interpretation*. New Haven: Yale University Press, 1971, xv + 573 p. [5]

Ricoeur, P. The atheism of Freudian psychoanalysis. *Concilium*, 1966, *16*, 59-72. [5]

Rieff, P. *Freud: The Mind of the Moralist*. New York: Viking Press, 1959. [5]

Rieff, P. The meaning of history and religion in Freud's thought. In B. Mazlish (Ed.) *Psychoanalysis and History*. Englewood Cliffs, New Jersey: Prentice-Hall, 1963. [5]

Rieff, P. *The Triumph of the Therapeutic*. New York: Harper and Row, 1966. [5]

Riesman, D. Freud: Religion as neurosis. *University of Chicago Round Table*, 1950, No. 638, 13-20. [5]

Ricsman, D. Freud, religion and science. *American Scholar*, 1951, *20*, 267-276. [5]

Riklin, F. *Wishfulfillment and Symbolism in Fairy Tales*. New York: Nervous and Mental Diseases Publishing Company, 1915. [27]

Rizzuto, A. M. Object relations and the formation of the image of God. *British Journal of Medical Psychology*, 1974, *47*, 83-99. [28, 35]

Roback, A. A. Freudian psychology and Jewish commentators of the Bible. *Jewish Forum*, 1918, *1*, 528-533. [26]

Roback, A. A. Is psychoanalysis a Jewish movement? *B'nai B.rith Magazine*, 1926, *40*, 118-119, 129-130, 198-201, 238-239. [26]

Robert, M. *From Oedipus to Moses.* Garden City, New York: Doubleday, 1977. [26]

Roberts, D. E. *Psychotherapy and a Christian View of Man.* New York: Scribner's, 1953. [39]

Roheim, G. *Australian Totemism: A Psycho-Analytic Study in Anthropology.* London: Allen and Unwin, 1925, 487 p. [17, 36]

Roheim, G. The gods of primitive man and the religion of the Andamanesian pygmies. *The Psychoanalytic Review*, 1928, *15*, 105-106. [17]

Roheim, G. Dying gods and puberty ceremonies. *Journal of the Royal Anthropological Institute*, 1929, *59*, 181-197. [8, 28, 32]

Roheim, G. *Animism, Magic and the Divine King.* New York: Knopf, 1930, xviii + 390 p. [17, 28]

Roheim, G. Animism and religion. *The Psychoanalytic Quarterly*, 1932, *1*, 59-112. [28]

Roheim, G. Primitive high gods. *The Psychoanalytic Quarterly*, 1934, *3*, 1-133. [17, 28]

Roheim, G. *The Riddle of the Sphinx.* London: The Hogarth Press, 1934. [27, 32]

Roheim, G. The covenant of Abraham. *The International Journal of Psycho-analysis*, 1939, *20*, 452-459. [24]

Roheim, G. The Garden of Eden. *Psychoanalytic Review*, 1940, *27*, 1-26, 177-199. [24]

Roheim, G. The psycho-analytic interpretation of culture. *International Journal of Psychoanalysis*, 1941, *22*, 147-169. [5]

Roheim, G. Myth and folk tale. *American Imago*, 1941, *2*, 266-279. [27]

Roheim, G. Transition rites. *Psychoanalytic Quarterly*, 1942, *11*, 336-374. [32]

Roheim, G. Aphrodite, or the woman with a penis. *Psychoanalytic Quarterly*, 1945, *14*, 350-390. [27]

Roheim, G. Saint Agatha and the Tuesday woman. *Inter-*

national *Journal of Psycho-Analysis*, 1946, *27*, 119-126. [10]

Roheim, G. *Psychoanalysis and Anthropology.* New York: International Universities Press, 1950. [28]

Roheim, G. The Oedipus complex, magic and culture. *Psychoanalysis and the Social Sciences*, 1950, *2*, 173-228. [5, 28]

Roehim, G. Mythology of Arnhem Land. *American Imago*, 1951, *8*, 181-187. [17]

Roheim, G. The panic of the gods. *The Psychoanalytic Quarterly*, 1952, *21*, 92-106. [8, 27]

Roheim, G. Some aspects of Semitic monotheism. *Psychoanalysis and the Social Sciences*, 1955, *4*, 169-222. [20, 22, 23]

Roheim, G. *The Origin and Function of Culture.* Garden City, New York: Doubleday, 1951, 146 p. [28]

Rosenfeld, E. M. The pan-headed Moses - A parallel. *International Journal of Psychoanalysis*, 1951, *32*, 83-93. [24]

Rosenzweig, E. M. Some notes, historical and psychoanalytical, on the people of Israel and the land of Israel with special reference to Deuteronomy. *American Imago*, 1940, *1*, 50-64. [20, 24]

Rosenzweig, E. M. Minister and congregation - a study in ambivalence. *Psychoanalytic Review*, 1941, *28*, 218-227. [30]

Ross, J. H. A current psychoanalytic concept of God. *International Record of Medicine*, 1955, 168, 760-767. [38]

Ross, N. Psychoanalysis and religion. *Journal of the American Psychoanalytic Association*, 1958, *6*, 519-539. [5]

Ross, N. Beyond "The future of an illusion." *Journal of the Hillside Hospital*, 1968, *17*, 259-276. [5]

de Rougemont, D. *The Devil's Share: An Essay on the Diabolic in Modern Society.* New York: Meridian Books, 1956. [5]

Roychoudhuri, A. K. Sita myth of the Ramayana. *Samiksa*, 1954, *8*, 235-243. [9]

Rubenstein, R. L. The significance of castration anxiety in Rabbinic mythology. *The Psychoanalytic Review*, 1963, *50*, 289-312. [24]

Rubenstein, R. L. A note on the research lag in psychoanalytic studies in religion. *Jewish Social Studies*, 1963, *25*, 133-144. [5]

Rubenstein, R. L. Freud and Judaism: A review article. *Journal of Religion*, 1967, *47*, 39-44. [26]

Rubenstein, R. L. *The Religious Imagination*. New York: Bobbs-Merrill, 1967, 256 p. [24]

Rubins, J. L. Neurotic attitudes toward religion. *American Journal of Psychoanalysis*, 1955, *15*, 71-81. [30, 31]

Runestam, A. *Psychoanalysis and Christitanity* (Tr. Winfield, O.) Rock Island, Illinois: Augustana Press, 1958, 194 p. [38]

Sachs, H. At the gates of heaven. *American Imago*, 1947, *4*, 15-32. [10]

Sachs, H. The transformation of impulses into the obsessional ritual. *American Imago*, 1946 *3*, 67-74. [32]

Saffady, W. Fears of sexual license during the English Reformation. *History of Childhood Quarterly*, 1973, *1*, 89-96. [10, 31]

Saffady, W. The effects of childhood bereavement and parental remarriage in sixteenth century England: The case of Thomas More. *History of Childhood Quarterly*, 1973, *1*, 310-336. [30]

Saffady, W. New developments in the psychoanalytic study of religion: A bibliographic survey of the literature since 1960. *The Psychoanalytic Review*, 1976, *63*, 291-299. [1, 2, 5]

Salzman, L. The psychology of religious and ideological conversion. *Psychiatry*, 1953, *16*, 177-187. [31]

Salzman, L. Psychology of (regressive) religious conversion. *Journal of Pastoral Care*, 1954, *8*, 61-75. [31]

Sanders, B. G. *Christianity after Freud; An Interpretation of the Christian Experience in the Light of Psycho-Analytic*

*Theory*. London: Bles, 1949. New York: Macmillan, 1949, 157 p. [38]

Sapirstein, M. R. The meaning of personal religious experience. Noveck, S. (Ed.) *Judaism and Psychiatry*, 119-127. [38]

Sarnoff, C. A. Mythic symbols in two precolumbian myths. *American Imago*, 1969, 26, 3-20. [7]

Schendler, D. Judas, Oedipus, and various saints. *Psychoanalysis*, 1954, 2, 41-46. [14]

Schick, A. The Jew as a sacrificial victim. *Psychoanalytic Review*, 1971, 58, 75-89. [10, 20]

Schlesinger, K. Origins of the Passover Seder in ritual sacrifice. *The Psychoanalytic Study of Society*, 1976, 7, 369-399. [23, 25]

Schlossman, H. H. Circumcision as defense: A study in psychoanalysis and religion. *The Psychoanalytic Quarterly*, 1966, 35, 340-356. [25]

Schlossman, H. God the father and his sons. *American Imago*, 1972, 8, 35-51. [20, 28]

Schmidberg, W. Original sin. *Psychoanalytic Review*, 1950, 37, 140-142. [28]

Schmidl, F. Problems of method in applied psychoanalysis. *Psychoanalytic Quarterly*, 1972, 41, 402-419. [5]

Schnaper, N. and Schnaper, H. W. A few kind words for the devil. *Journal of Religion and Health*, 1969, 8, 107-122. [38]

Schneck, J. M. Freud and Kronos. *American Journal of Psychiatry*, 1968, 125, 629-693. [18]

Schneiderman, L. Psychological evolution from polytheism to monotheism. *The Psychoanalytic Review*, 1964, 51, 274-284. [20]

Schneiderman, L. A theory of repression in the light of archaic religion. *The Psychoanalytic Review*, 1966, 53, 220-232. [18, 28, 32]

Schneiderman, L. The cult of Osiris in relation to primitive initiation rites. *The Psychoanalytic Review*, 1965, 52, 28-50. [8]

Schnier, J. The Tibetan Lamaist ritual: Chod. *International Journal of Psycho-Analysis*, 1957, *38*, 402-407. [9]

Schoedfeld, C. G. God the father and mother: Study and extension of Freud's conception of God as an exalted father. *American Imago*, 1962, *19*, 213-234. [28]

Schoenfeld, C. G. Psychoanalysis and anti-semitism. *The Psychoanalytic Review*, 1966, *53*, 24-37. [20, 22]

Schroeder, T., Rev. S.C. Religious "Love in Action" (Introduction and interpolations). *Psychoanalytic Review*, 1925, *12*, 414-419. [31]

Schroeder, T. A contribution to the psychology of religion: The French prophets and John Lacy. *The Psychoanalytic Review*, 1925, *12*, 16-29. [16, 28]

Schroeder, T. Manufacturing "The Experience of God." *Psychoanalytic Review*, 1927, *14*, 71-84. [31]

Schroeder, T. Guilt and inferiority as creator of religious experience. *The Psychoanalytic Review*, 1929, *16*, 46-54. [10, 28]

Schroeder, T. The psychoanalytic approach to religious experience. *Psychoanalytic Review*, 1929, *16*, 361-376. [31]

Schroeder, T. A "living God" Incarnate. *Psychoanalytic Review*, 1932, *19*, 36-46. [30]

Schuster, D. B. The Holly Communion: An historical and psychoanalytical study. *The Bulletin of the Philadelphia Association for Psychoanalysis*, 1970, *20*, 223-236. [15]

Segal, B. Serpent - staffs of antiquity. *Hebrew Medical Journal*, 1963, *2*, 229-231. [24]

Seidenberg, R. Sacrificing the first you see. *The Psychoanalytic Review*, 1966, *53*, 49-62. [24]

Sereno, R. Some observations on the Santa Claus Custom. *Psychiatry*, 1951, *14*, 387-396. [13]

Sessions, P. M. Ego religion and superego religion in alcoholics. *Quarterly Journal of Studies on Alcohol*, 1957, *18*, 121-125. [30]

Shaw, D. The Christian roots of psychoanalysis. In *Chrisianity and Modern Man*. Washington, 1952, 51-66. [38]

Sherman, M. H. Values, religion and the psychoanalyst. *Journal of Social Psychology*, 1957, *45*, 261-269. [5]

Siegel, L. M. A bar to conversion. *The Psychoanalytic Review*, 1966, *53*, 16-23. [20]

Siegman, A. W. An empirical investigation of the psychoanalytic theory of religious behavior. *Journal for the Scientific Study of Religion*, 1961, *1*, 74-78. [37]

Sillman, L. R. Monotheism and the sense of reality. *International Journal of Psychoanalysis*, 1949, *30*, 124-132. [5, 20]

de Silva, M. W. P. *Buddhist and Freudian Psychology*. Colombo: Lake House Investment, 1973. [9]

Silverberg, W. V. Psychoanalysis, religion, and world crisis. *Holy Cross Magazine*, 1942, *53*, 195-198. [38]

Skeels, D. R. Eros and thanatos in Nex Perce river mythology. *American Imago*, 1964, *21*, 103-110. [7]

Skinner, J. Ritual matricide: A study of the origins of sacrifice. *American Imago*, 1961, *18*, 71-102. [32]

Slap, J. W. The genesis of Moses. *Psychoanalytic Quarterly*, 1958, *27*, 400-402. [24]

Slochower, H. The Book of Job: The Hebrew myth of the chosen God, its symbolism and psychoanalytic process. *International Record of Medicine*, 1958, *171*, 761-769. [24]

Slochower, H. *Mythopoesis*. Detroit: Wayne State University Press, 1970. [27]

Slochower, H. Psychoanalytic distinction between myth and mythopoesis. *Journal of the American Psychoanalytic Association*, 1970, *18*, 150-164. [27]

Smith, G. E. Freud's speculations in ethnology. *Monist*, 1923, *33*, 81-97. [28]

Smith, P. Luther's early development in the light of psychoanalysis. *American Journal of Psychology*, 1913, *24*, 360-377. [30]

Smith, V. E. The study of man: An essay in reconstruction. In Braceland, J. J., *Faith, Reason, and Modern Psychiatry*. New York: Kennedy, 1955, 145-179. [38]

Spencer, K. *Mythology and Values. An Analysis of Navaho Chantway Myths.* Philadelphia: American Folklore Society, 1957, 240 p. [7]

Spinks, G. S. *Psychology and Religion: An Introduction to Contemporary Views.* Boston: Beacon Press, 1965, xv + 221 p. [5]

Spiro, M. E. and D'Andrade, R. G. A cross-cultural study of some supernatural beliefs. *American Anthropologist*, 1960, *60*, 456-466. [27, 37]

Spiro, M. E. Religious systems as culturally constituted defense mechanisms. In author's *Context and Meaning in Cultural Anthropology*. New York: Free Press, 1965, 100-113. [27]

Spitz, R. A. The genesis of magical and transcendent cults. *American Imago*, 1973, *29*, 1 - 10. [28]

Steinbach, A. A. Can psychiatry and religion meet? In Noveck, S. (Ed.) *Judaism and Psychiatry*, 169-176. [38]

Steinletz, E. Hassidism and psychoanalysis. *Judaism*, 1960, *9*, 222-229. [26]

Stephane, A. *L'univers Contestationnaire, ou les Nouveaux Chretiens: Etude Psychoanalytique* (The Universe in Contention, or the New Christians: Psychoanalytic Study). Paris: Payot, 1969. [5]

Sterba, R. A Dutch celebration of a festival. *American Imago*, 1941, *2*, 205-208. [13]

Sterba, R. On Christmas. *Psychoanalytic Quarterly*, 1944, *13*, 79-83. [13]

Sterba, R. On Hallowe'en. *American Imago*, 1948, *5*, 213-224. [13]

Stern, K. *The Third Revolution. A Study of Psychiatry and*

*Religion.* New York: Harcourt Brace, 1954, 306 p. [38]

Stern, K. Psychiatry and religion. *Hospital Progress* (St. Louis), 1955, *36*, 62-63. [38]

Stern, K. Some spiritual aspects of psychotherapy. In Braceland, F. J. *Faith, Reason and Modern Psychiatry.* New York: Kennedy, 1955, 125-140. [38]

Stern, M. M. Ego psychology, myth, and rite: Remarks about the relationship of the individual and the group. *The Psychoanalytic Study of Society*, 1964, *3*, 71-93. [27, 32, 34]

Stevenson, I. P. Assumptions of religion and psychiatry. *Bulletin of the Menninger Clinic*, 1955, *19*, 199-209. [38]

Stokes, A. *Greek Culture and the Ego.* London: Tavistock, 1958, 101 p. [18]

Strachey, J. Preliminary notes upon the problem of Aknaten. *International Journal of Psychoanalysis*, 1939, *20*, 33-42. [8]

Strunk, O. Perceived relationships between parental and deity concepts. *Psychological Newsletter*, 1959, *10*, 222-226. [37]

Strunk, O., Jr. (Ed.) *Readings in the Psychology of Religion.* New York: Abingdon Press, 1959, 288 p. [5]

Stunkard, A. S. Some interpersonal aspects of an oriental religion. *Psychiatry*, 1951, *14*, 419-431. [9]

Sullivan, J. J. Two psychologies and the study of religion. *Journal for the Scientific Study of Religion*, 1961 - 62, *1*, 155-164. [5]

Sun, J. T. Psychology in primitive Buddhism. *The Psychoanalytic Review*, 1924, *11*, 39-47. [9]

Sutherland, R. L. The pastor and the metnal health team. *Journal of Religion and Health*, 1964, *4*, 22. [39]

Sutherland, R. L. Therapeutic goals and ideals of health. *Journal of Religion and Health*, 1964, *3*, 119. [39]

Suttie, I. D. Religion, racial character and mental and social health. *British Journal of Medical Psychology*, 1932, *12*, 289-314. [10, 29]

Suzuki, D. T., Fromm, E. and De Martino, R. *Zen Buddhism and Psychoanalysis.* New York: Harper, 1960, viii + 180 p. [9]

Suzuki, D. T. (Ed.) *Zen Buddhism and Psychoanalysis.* New York: Grove Press, 1963. [9]

Swisher, W. S. *Religion and the New Psychology, a Psycho-Analytic Study of Religion.* Boston: Marshall Jones, 1920, xv + 261 p. London: Routledge, 1920, 286 p. [5]

Tamayo, A. and Desjardines, L. Belief systems and conceptual images of parents and God. *Journal of Psychology*, 1976, 92, 131-140. [37]

Tarachow, S. Totem feast in modern dress. *American Imago*, 1948, 5, 65 - 72. [15]

Tarachow, S. Applied psychoanalysis. II. Religion. In *Annual Survey of Psychoanalysis*, 1950, 1, 312-317. [2]

Tarachow, S. Mythology. In Frosch, J. (Ed.) *The Annual Survey of Psychoanalysis*, 1950, 1, 317-321. [2]

Tarachow, S. Applied psychoanalysis: Mythology and folklore. In Frosch, J. (Ed.) *The Annual Survey of Psychoanalysis*, 1951, 2, 553-567. [2]

Tarachow, S. Applied psychoanalysis: Religion and mythology. In Frosch, J. (Ed.) *The Annual Survey of Psychoanalysis*, 1952, 3, 494-511. [2]

Tarachow, S. St. Paul and early Christianity. A psychoanalytic and historical study. In Muensterberger, W. and Axelrad, S. *Psychoanalysis and the Social Sciences.* New York: International Universities Press, 1955, 4, 223-282. [10]

Tarachow, S. Judas, the beloved executioner. *The Psychoanalytic Quarterly*, 1960, 29, 528-554. [14]

Tarachow, S. Mythology and ego psychology. *The Psychoanalytic Study of Society*, 1964, 3, 9-12. [27, 34]

Tarachow, S. Ambiguity and human imperfection. *Journal of the American Psychoanalytic Association*, 1965, 13, 85-101. [27, 32]

Taubes, J. Religion and the future of psychoanalysis. *Psycho-*

*analysis*, 1956-57, *4-5*, 136-142. [5]

Teslaar, J. S. Van The theogeny of "El" (A biblical instance of purposive condensation). *Psyche and Eros*, 1920, *1*, 114-117. [24]

Theodoropoulus, J. "Adam's Rib." *The Psychoanalytic Review*, 1967, *54*, 150-152. [24]

Thouless, R. H. A difference between religion and neurosis. In Strunk, O., Jr. (Ed.) *Readings in the Psychology of Religion*. Nashville, Tennessee: Abingdon Press, 1959, 228. From Author's *An Introduction to the Psychology of Religion*. London: Cambridge University Press, 277-278. [28]

Thrift, I. E. Religion and madness. The case of William Cowper. *Psychoanalytic Review*, 1926, *13*, 312-317. [30]

Tillich, P. J. The religious symbol (Tr.: Adams, J. L. and Fraenkel, E.) *Daedalus*, 1958, *87*, 3-21. In May, R. *Symbolism in Religion and Literature*. New York: G. Braziller, 1960, 75-98. [5]

Tillich, P. The meaning of health. *Perspectives of Biology and Medicine*, 1961, *5*, 92-100. In Belgum, D. *Religion and Medicine*. Ames, Iowa: Iowa State University Press, 1967, 3-12. [39]

Trevett, L. D. Origin of the creation myth: A hypothesis. *Journal of the American Psychoanalytic Association*, 1957, *5*, 461-468. [28]

Troisiers, J. Menhirs, trilithons and dolmens: Their symbolism. *British Journal of Medical Psychology*, 1932, *12*, 337-342. [29]

Trueblood, D. E. The challenge of Freud. *Pastoral Psychology*, 1958, *9*, 37-44. [39]

Turner, J. E. Freud and the illusion of religion. *Journal of Religion*, 1933, *11*, 212-221. [5]

Vander Veldt, J. H. and Odenwald, R. P. *Psychiatry and Catholicism*. New York, Toronto, London: McGraw Hill, 1952, 433 p. [38]

Vergote, A. et al. Concept of God and parental images.

*Journal for the Scientific Study of Religion,* 1969, *8,* 79-87. [37]

Vergote, A. and Aubert, C. Parental images and representations of God. *Social Compass,* 1972, *19,* 431-444. [37]

Veszy-Wagner, I. An Irish legend as proof of Freud's theory of joint parricide. *International Journal of Psychoanalysis,* 1957, *38,* 117-120. [28]

Vetter, G. B. *Magic and Religion: Their Psychological Nature, Origin, and Fuction.* New York: Philosophical Library, 1958, 555 p. [5]

Vollmerhausen, J. W. Religion, perfectionism and the fair deal. *American Journal of Psychoanalysis,* 1965, *25,* 203-215. [28]

Walker, K. Psychology and religion. *Hibbert Journal,* 1961, *60,* 10-15. [38]

Wallace, E. R. The psychodynamic determinants of *Totem and Taboo. Psychiatry,* 1977, *40,* 79-87. [24, 26]

Walsh, M. N. A psychoanalytic interpretation of a primitive dramatic ritual. *Journal of the Hillside Hospital,* 1962, *11,* 3 - 20. [7, 17]

Walters, O. S. Metaphysics, religion and psychotherapy. *Journal of Counseling Psychology,* 1958, *5,* 243 - 252. [38]

Walters, O. S. Theology and changing concepts of the unconscious. *Religion in Life,* 1968, *37,* 112-128. [38]

Want, R. L. Psychoanalysis and religion. *Australia Journal of Psychologic Philosophy,* 1939, *17,* 241-250. [38]

Ware, J. G. "Greater still is Diana of the Ephesians." *American Imago,* 1962, *19,* 253-275. [18]

Watkins, J. G. Concerning Freud's paper on "The Moses of Michaelangelo." *American Imago,* 1951, *8,* 61-63. [11]

Watson, A. S. The fear of faith. *Pastoral Psychology,* 1963, *139,* 18-26. [39]

Watson, G. A psychologist's view of religious symbols. In Johnson, F. E. *Religious Symbolism.* New York: Institute for Religious and Social Studies, Harper, 1955, 117-127. [27]

Wayne, R. Prometheus and Christ. *Psychoanalysis and the Social Sciences*, 1951, *3*, 201-219. [14, 18]

Wayne, R. A little religious ceremonial. *American Imago*, 1954, *11*, 194-202. [15, 32]

Weigert, E. V. The cult and mythology of the Magna Mater from the standpoint of psychoanalysis. *Psychiatry*, 1938, *1*, 347-378. [8]

Weigert, E. V. The contribution of pastoral counseling and psychotherapy to mental health. *British Journal of Medical Psychology*, 1960, *33*, 269-273. [39]

Weininger, B. The interpersonal factor in the religious experience. *Psychoanalysis, Journal of the National Psychological Association for Psychoanalysis*, 1955, *3*, 27-44. [31]

Weisner, W. M. and Riffel, R. P. A. Scrupulosity: Religion and obsessive compulsive behavior in children. *American Journal of Psychiatry*, 1960, *117*, 314-318. [30]

Weiss, S. A. The Biblical story of Ruth: Analytic implications of the Hebrew masoretic text. *American Imago*, 1949, *16*, 195-209. [24]

Wellisch, E. *Isaac and Oedipus: A Study in Biblical Psychology of the Sacrifice of Isaac, the Akedah.* London: Routledge and Kegan Paul, 1954, 131 p. [24]

Wells, F. L. The beans of St. Botolph's : And other letters to Screwtape. *American Imago*, 1948, *5*, 38-64. [5]

Westendrop, F. The value of Freud's illusion. *Journal of Psychology and Theology*, 1975 (Spring), *3*, 82-89. [38]

Wilbur, G. B. Soul belief and psychology. *The Psychoanalytic Review*, 1932, *19*, 319-326. [28]

Wilc, I. S. Psychoanalysis and religion. *Mental Hygiene*, 1932, *16*, 529-563. [5, 38]

Winnicott, D. W. *The Maturational Processes and the Facilitating Environment.* New York: International Universities Press, 1965. [35]

Wisdom, J. O. Gods. In Wisdom, J. O. *Philosophy and Psycho-Analysis.* London: Blackwell, 1952, 149-168. [5]

Witcutt, W. P. *Catholic Thought and Modern Psychology.* London: Burns, Oates and Washbourne, 1943, 1944, 57 p. [38]

Wittels, F. Psychoanalysis and history: The Nibelungs and the Bible. *The Psychoanalytic Quarterly*, 1946, *15*, 88-103. [27]

Wittels, F. A contribution to a symposium on religious art and literature. *Journal of the Hillside Hospital*, 1952, *1*, 3-6. [31]

Wolf, R. Castration symbolism in patrisitic thought: Preliminary studies in the development of Christianity. *Psychoanalysis and the Psychoanalytic Review*, 1962, *49*, 26-38. [10]

de Wolf, M. J. Comments on Freud and Kronos. *Psychoanalytic Quarterly*, 1972, *41*, 420-423. [18]

Wolff, W. *Changing Concepts of the Bible. A Psychological Analysis of the Word, Symbols and Beliefs.* New York: Hermitage House, 1951, 473 p. [38]

Wolff, W. Symposium on psychiatry and religion. Introdution. *International record of Medicine*, 1955, *168*, 767-768. [38]

Wolff, W. (Ed.) *Psychiatry and Religion.* New York: MD Publications, 1956, 62 p. [38]

Wolff, W. Introduction to the symposium on psychiatry and religion. In author's *Psychiatry and Religion*, 1-2. [38]

Wolff, W. Freud the Jew. *Jewish Spectator.* New York, 1958 (May), 27. [26]

Wolman, B. B. (Ed.) *Pscychoanalysis andCatholicism.* New York: Gardner Press, 1976. [38]

Woodward, L. E. Fostering mental health through the church program. In Maves, P. B. *The Church and Metal Health.* New York, London: Scribner's 1953, 129-157. [38]

Woolf, M. Prohibitions against the simultaneous consumption of milk and flesh in Orthodox Jewish laws. *International Journal of Psycho-Analysis*, 1945, *26*, 169-177. [22]

Woollcott, P. Some considerations of creativity and religious experience in St. Augustine of Hippo. *Journal for the Scientific Study of Religion*, 1966, *5*, 273-283. [30]

Young, D. R. Pastoral counseling in the church? *Journal of Religion and Health*, 1964, *3*, 353 - 358. [39]

Young, F. W. *Initiation Ceremonies: A Cross-Cultural Study of Status Dramatization.* Indianapolis: Bobbs-Merrill, 1965, xiv + 199 p. [32]

Zeckel, A. The totemistic significance of the unicorn. In Wilbur, G. and Muensterberger, W. (Eds.) *Psychoanalysis and Culture.* New York: International Universities Press, 1951, 344 - 360. [27]

Zeligs, D. F. Psychological factors in the teaching of Bible stories. *Jewish Education*, 1951, *22*, 24-28. [24]

Zeligs, D. F. Two episodes in the life of Jacob. *American Imago*, 1953, *10*, 181 - 205. [24]

Zeligs, D. Abraham and monotheism. *American Imago*, 1954, *11*, 293-316. [24]

Zeligs, D. F. The personality of Joseph. *American Imago*, 1955, *12*, 47-69. [24]

Zeligs, D. F. A character study of Samuel. *American Imago*, 1955, *12*, 355-386. [24]

Zeligs, D. F. A psychoanalytic note on the function of the Bible. *American Imago*, 1957, *14*, 57-60. [24]

Zeligs, D. F. Saul, the tragic king. *American Imago*, 1957, *4*, 61-100. [24]

Zeligs, D. F. The mother in Hebraic Monotheism. *The Psychoanalytic Study of Society*, 1960, *1*, 287-311. [24]

Zeligs, D. F. A study of King David. *American Imgao*, 1960, *17*, 179-200. [24]

Zeligs, D. F. Solomon: Man and myth. *Psychoanalysis and the Psychoanalytic Review*, 1961, *48*, 77-103, 91-110. [24]

Zeligs, D. F. The family romance of Moses. I. The "personal myth." *American Imago*, 1966, *23*, 110-131. [24]

Zeligs, D. F. Moses in Midian: The burning bush. *American*

*Imago*, 1969, *26*, 379-400. [24]

Zeligs, D. F. Moses and Pharaoh: A psychoanalytic study of their encounter. *American Imago*, 1973, *30*, 129-220. [24]

Zeligs, D. F. *Psychoanalysis and the Bible*. New York: Bloch Publishing Co., 1974. [24]

Zilboorg, G. A response. *Psychoanalytic Quarterly*, 1944, *13*, 93-100. [38]

Zilboorg, G. Psychiatry and religion. *Atlantic Monthly*, 1949, *183* (January), 47-50. [38]

Zilboorg, G. *Psychoanalysis and Religion*. New York: Barnes and Noble, 1950. [38]

Zilboorg, G. Scientific psychotherapy and religious issues. *Theological Studies*, 1953, *14*, 288-297. *Journal of Mental Science*, 1954, *100*, 402-410. [39]

Zilboorg, G. Some denials and assertations of religious faith. In Braceland, F. J. *Faith, Reason and Modern Psychiatry*. New York: Kennedy, 1955, 99-121. [39]

Zilboorg, G. Is religion a cure for neurosis? *Bulletin Guild of Catholic Psychiatrists*, 1958, *6*, (1). [39]

Zilboorg, G. *Freud and Religion: A Restatement of an Old Controversy*. Westminster, Maryland: Newman Press. London: Geoffrey Chapman, 1958, 65 p. [38]

Zilboorg, G. Psychoanalysis and religion. *Pastoral Psychology*, 1959, *10*, 41-48. [38]

Zilboorg, G. *Psychoanalysis and Religion* (Ed.: Zilboorg, M. S.) New York: Farrar, Straus and Cudahy, 1962, xi + 243 p. [38]

Zimmerman, F. Origin and significance of the Jewish rite of circumcision. *Psychoanalytic Review*, 1951, *38*, 103 - 112. [25]

RAYMOND H. FOGLER LIBRARY
DATE DUE

BOOKS ARE SUBJECT TO
RECALL AFTER TWO WEEKS